VAIN ENDEAVOR

DUKE HISTORICAL PUBLICATIONS

VAIN ENDEAVOR

Robert Lansing's Attempts To End The American-Japanese Rivalry

BURTON F. BEERS

Duke University Press *Durham, N. C.* *1962*

Library of Congress catalog card number 61-16907
Cambridge University Press, London N.W.1, England

Printed in the United States of America
by the Seeman Printery, Inc., Durham, N. C.

For my Mother and Father

This book has been published with the assistance of funds from a grant to the Duke University Press by the Ford Foundation.

Preface

The Far Eastern policy of Woodrow Wilson's administration is the subject of solid historical studies. Among leading monographs are the following: Tien-yi Li, *Woodrow Wilson's China Policy, 1913-1917* (New York, 1952); Russell H. Fifield, *Woodrow Wilson and the Far East: The Diplomacy of the Shantung Question* (New York, 1952); Betty Miller Unterberger, *America's Siberian Expedition, 1918-1920: A Study of National Policy* (Durham, 1956); and Roy W. Curry, *Woodrow Wilson and Far Eastern Policy, 1913-1921* (New York, 1957). To these volumes may be added studies which have been done as part of broader works, such as, for example, chapters in Professor Arthur Link's several volumes on Wilson, or Professor George Kennan's on American-Russian relations. While all of these studies vary in scope and the context in which they deal with Far Eastern affairs, they have in common one feature: the narratives focus on President Wilson; or, to state the matter another way, the historical record of American Far Eastern policy is set forth primarily in terms of Wilson's hopes, accomplishments, and failures.

Robert Lansing, rather than Wilson, is central to the narrative that follows. As State Department Counselor and Secretary of State, Lansing developed ideas for dealing with Far Eastern problems which were uniquely his own and which he sought to incorporate into official American policy. Although these aspects of Lansing's activity have received little attention, they form an important part of the historical record.

In the first place, a narrative dealing with Lansing furnishes explanations of some apparent inconsistencies in the Wilson diplomacy. For example, in January, 1917, Lansing told the Japanese Ambassador that the United States recognized informally Japan's "special interests" in Shantung. Such a statement was contrary to the established policy of opposing these Japanese claims. Lansing's remarks, however, did not result from ignorance or carelessness. Rather, the Secretary was speaking independently with the aim of laying the groundwork for an American bargain with Japan, a bargain of which the President was not yet informed. Since existing studies have largely overlooked this and other efforts by Lansing to change the President's Far Eastern policy, this volume will help to complete the historical record.

But an even more important purpose is to provide fresh interpretations of Wilson's Far Eastern policy. Thus far Wilson's policy has been appraised largely in terms of the extent to which the President was successful in achieving his objectives. In this study new standards of measurement will be introduced. The line pursued by Wilson will be compared with alternatives proposed by Lansing. To illustrate how this comparison affects a judgment of Wilson's policy, the Shantung controversy at the Paris Peace Conference of 1919 may be cited. Wilson believed that the controversy presented him with a hard choice: An American refusal to accept the Japanese claims would result in a victory on behalf of the principle of China's integrity but would be followed by a Japanese decision to boycott the League of Nations; concessions to the Japanese claims, on the other hand, would be a blow to the President's aims in the Orient but would keep Japan in the League. Historians, sifting the evidence upon which Wilson based his thinking, have generally approved Wilson's decision to sacrifice immediate advantages in Shantung in favor of the League. Lansing, however, viewed the choice another way. After examining sources of the Japanese claims on Shantung, the Secretary decided that concessions to these claims would encourage Japan to follow an independent and militant line in East Asia. Japan might join the League, but she could not be relied upon to co-operate in keeping the peace. Nor would she be likely to work with the United States in developing the new banking consortium in China or measures for coping with the Bolshevik revolution in Siberia. In consequence, Lansing questioned the soundness of Wilson's decision. The present study, having investigated the prospects outlined by Lansing, concludes that there is reason to modify existing evaluations of Wilson's decision. Other reinterpretations are set forth on such episodes as American diplomacy with respect to the Twenty-one Demands, Lansing-Ishii negotiations, Siberian intervention, and negotiations looking toward the establishment of the second consortium.

In an earlier form the present study was a doctoral dissertation entitled, "Robert Lansing and the Far East, 1914-1917" (Duke University, 1956). Additional research, which extended the scope of the study to 1920, was financed largely by two grants from the

North Carolina State College Faculty Research and Professional Development Fund.

Research was an adventure in helpfulness. I am indebted to Mrs. Edith Bolling Wilson for permission to make use of the President's papers; to Mrs. Bainbridge Colby for permission to use her husband's papers; to the family of Henry White for permission to use the White Papers; and to the Yale University Library and Graduate School for permission to use the House, Polk, and Auchincloss Papers. The staffs of the North Carolina State College Library; Duke University Library; Collection of Regional History, Cornell University; Sterling Memorial Library, Yale University; Manuscripts Division, Library of Congress; and Foreign Affairs Section, National Archives, were unfailingly courteous and helpful. A special expression of thanks goes to Miss Gertrude Helmer, Watertown, New York, who did so much to make enjoyable and worthwhile my journeys to Lansing's home town, and who is herself a boundless source of lore about the region in which she lives. To Miss Nama Washburn, also of Watertown, go my thanks for inviting my wife and me into her home for an evening's discussion of the Fortnightly Club and its members. Mrs. Seymore Jones, again of Watertown, located a chest of pertinent materials in her attic and permitted me to examine it. And finally, it is appropriate here to recall the many kindnesses of Robert Lansing's late sister, Miss Emma Sterling Lansing, and cousin, Mrs. John L. Gill. By allowing me to visit them in the old Lansing home and reminiscing for many hours about their family, these two ladies provided insights which could not be obtained from the written record.

Dr. Paul H. Clyde directed the early stages of my research while I was a graduate student and was kind enough to read a late draft of the manuscript during a busy summer. Whatever merit this study may have is due largely to his counsel. To Dr. Dorothy Borg, I am indebted for the time that she took to read and criticize the entire study. Portions of the volume were presented in a seminar in American Far Eastern policy at Harvard University. To Dr. Harold Vinacke, who conducted the seminar, and members of the seminar, I am indebted for helpful suggestions. None of these scholars, of course, is responsible for errors which may appear.

It would not be fitting to close these acknowledgments without expressing thanks to my wife, Pauline Cone Beers. Her special knowledge of archives and archival procedure assisted my research, and she performed cheerfully the innumerable technical tasks which seem to be the inevitable lot of the historian's wife.

B. F. B.

Contents

VAIN ENDEAVOR

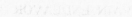

1. A "Book Lawyer" Becomes A Diplomat

Robert Lansing's place in the history of American Far Eastern policy deserves careful study. Appointed in 1914 as the State Department's Counselor and in 1915 as Secretary of State, Lansing held key posts in Woodrow Wilson's administration. In these posts he did not function simply as an executor of the President's policies. Rather, he sought the adoption of ideas which were frequently quite distinct from Wilson's. The significance of Lansing's activity derives partly from the imprint that it made on American diplomacy. Of even greater importance is the basis which Lansing's record provides for making a fresh evaluation of Wilson's Far Eastern policy. An understanding of Lansing's role begins with an inquiry into personal circumstances which affected his handling of Far Eastern affairs.

Lansing's association with the State Department maintained a family tradition for public service. Born on October 17, 1864, in Watertown, a small city in northern New York state, he was the eldest child of John and Maria Dodge Lansing. Through both parents Lansing was descended from families which had won distinction in state affairs. His maternal grandfather, Edwin Dodge, who settled near Watertown early in the nineteenth century, gained wealth and prestige as land agent for Gouverneur Morris. He also served in the State Legislature and as a judge in the state court system.[1] On the paternal side Lansing's ances-

[1] Interview with Miss Emma Sterling Lansing and Mrs. John L. Gill.

tors were Dutch families who settled near Albany in the colonial era. Lansing's great-great-grandfather, John Lansing, was a delegate to the Philadelphia Constitutional Convention, a member of the State Legislature, and Chancellor of New York. Another forebear, Jacob C. TenEyck, played a leading role in the revolt against the British and was later appointed Judge of the State Court of Common Pleas. Lansing's great-grandfather and grandfather were distinguished lawyers. His second cousin, Frederick Lansing, was state senator. His father was a successful attorney and was active in Watertown civic affairs.[2]

The family record made an impression on young "Bert" Lansing. He apparently never questioned that he was destined for a legal career. Nor did he doubt his ability to do what was required of him. As a young man, he took advantage methodically of the educational opportunities that were open to him. He was sent to a private grammar school and Watertown High School. He attended Amherst College, graduating from that institution in 1886. For the next three years he read law in his father's office. In 1889 he was admitted to the New York Bar, and, following the trip to Europe which customarily climaxed a gentleman's education, he became his father's law partner.

The young lawyer possessed characteristics which seemed to portend success. While Lansing was by no means brilliant, his intellectual abilities were substantial. Moreover, he was willing to work. Many years later his sister recalled that Lansing read constantly. She pictured him sitting night after night in his father's library with a book and pot of cold coffee. Indeed, in order to satisfy his desire to read, he resorted to invention. He devised a bracket for holding an oil lamp at the head of his bed

---

Watertown, N. Y., August 30, 1955. Hereinafter cited as Interview, 1955. *Watertown Daily Times,* Oct. 31, 1928.

[2] *Watertown Daily Times,* Oct. 31, 1928. *New York Times,* Oct. 31, 1928. Alexander C. Flick, ed., *History of the State of New York* (New York, 1933-1937), V, 31-61.

and a bookrack for the bathtub.[3] The subjects which most interested him were law, American history, and psychology.[4]

Later, as a member of the State Department, Lansing found his energy and intellectual capacity decided assets. Associates were impressed by his capacity for work and ability to absorb and retain vast quantities of complex material. Lansing's reading in psychology undoubtedly assisted him in the effort he was to make to analyze the President's mental processes and to devise ways of coping with their consequences. But as Lansing embarked upon a law career the qualities just described were offset in some measure by other characteristics. He was diffident, almost shy. He disliked contact with strangers and was reluctant to appear in court. His associates called him a "book lawyer" because of his custom of preparing a case and then turning it over to his father for presentation. John Lansing, a genial, outgoing person, was puzzled and sometimes irritated by his son's refusal to circulate among the townspeople in order to solicit business for the office.[5] Apparently Lansing recognized these difficulties for what they were and looked for a way to overcome them.

Happily an opportunity to enter a branch of law where he could make full use of his ability appeared shortly after he began his practice. Late in the 1880's Eleanor Foster, daughter of the veteran American diplomat, John Watson Foster, came to Watertown to visit her sister, Mrs. Allen Macy Dulles, Sr. Lansing met her and initiated a courtship which culminated in marriage in January, 1890.[6] Two years later he received from his father-in-law, who was then serving as Secretary of State under President Benjamin Harrison, an appointment as Associate Counsel for the United States in the Behring Fur Seal Arbitration. The appointment provided the young lawyer with

[3] Interview with Miss Emma Sterling Lansing. Watertown, N. Y., October 9, 1954. Hereinafter cited as Interview, 1954.

[4] "The Diplomatic Counsellor General of the United States in Anxious Times," *Current Opinion,* LVIII (April, 1915), 240.

[5] *New York Times,* October 31, 1928. Interview, 1955.

[6] Interview, 1954.

an introduction to international law, the practice of which was more congenial than work in Watertown. During the next fifteen years, Lansing engaged intermittently in the practice of international law. In 1896-1897 he served as American Counsel on the Behring Sea Claims Commission. He was appointed Solicitor and Counselor for the United States before the Alaskan Boundary Tribunal in 1903. Between these jobs he served as Counsel for the Mexican and Chinese Legations in Washington and represented private parties before Canadian and Venezuelan arbitral commissions.[7]

While carrying on these activities, Lansing maintained the connection with his father's office. This was due largely to his strong sense of family responsibility. The elder Lansing's sight failed late in life. However, his mind remained clear, and he continued to work. During these years, Lansing conducted his father to and from the office each day. The two men co-operated as they had done for many years. The association continued until John Lansing's death in 1907.[8] Only then did Lansing leave the Watertown office. He moved to Washington, where he joined his father-in-law in a practice dealing entirely with cases of an international character. This new partnership lasted until Lansing was appointed to the State Department seven years later.

These were busy years. Foster's governmental connections brought much business to the partners. Lansing continued to represent the State Department in various capacities. Between 1908 and 1914 he acted successively as Counsel in the North Atlantic Fisheries dispute, Technical Delegate to the Fur Seal Conference, Agent before the British-American Claims Commission, and Special Counsel to the State Department on a variety of questions.[9] Nor was this all. The appearance of per-

[7] "The Appointment of Mr. Robert Lansing of New York as Counselor in the Department of State," *American Journal of International Law,* VIII (April, 1914), 336-337. Hereinafter cited as "Appointment," *AJIL.*

[8] Interview, 1954.

[9] "Appointment," *AJIL,* VIII, 336-337.

sons concerned exclusively in the practice of international law was a recent development in America. Lansing was keenly interested in bringing organization to and advancing scholarly knowledge in his profession. With these purposes in mind he helped to found in 1907 the American Society of International Law. In the same year he co-operated with Dr. James Brown Scott in publishing the first issue of the *American Journal of International Law,* which was to be devoted to the publication of learned articles and reviews. Lansing himself served on the editorial staff and contributed occasionally to the journal.

Lansing's official career was affected by these years in Washington. The association with Foster brought prestige that was to figure heavily in his appointment to the State Department. A more subtle but no less important effect came from the tutoring in foreign affairs that he received from his father-in-law. Foster had had a long and varied diplomatic career. He had served as Minister to Mexico, Ambassador to Russia, Special Envoy to Spain as well as Secretary of State. Following his retirement from the latter post, he became Special Adviser to the Chinese Commission to negotiate peace at the end of the Sino-Japanese War. This appointment had provided the opportunity for travel in China and Japan. After Lansing moved to Washington he was constantly in contact with Foster. Not only were they law partners, but they shared the same house and took vacations together. While there are few documents extant to indicate the nature of this relationship, there can be little doubt that Lansing derived from it much of the substance and spirit of diplomacy.[10] For this reason it will be worthwhile to outline Foster's ideas concerning the conduct of American Far Eastern affairs.

Foster was convinced that in the twentieth century the United

[10] This idea was accepted by members of the Wilson administration. See Josephus Daniels, *The Wilson Era: Years of Peace—1910-1917* (Chapel Hill, N. C., 1944), p. 438. Hereinafter cited as Daniels, *Years of Peace.* Also Edith Bolling Wilson, *My Memoir* (Indianapolis, 1939), p. 64. Hereinafter cited as E. B. Wilson, *Memoir.*

States was destined to play an increasingly important part in the affairs of East Asia. The involvement would not stem from any moral duty to civilize and uplift the people of Japan and China. Rather, the United States would be concerned with markets. The industrial resources of the United States seemed to be expanding beyond the point where production could be absorbed in the domestic market. It was inevitable that manufacturers would seek customers in undeveloped countries such as the Philippines and China. A primary duty of the American government was to assist in this search for markets.

With respect to China the United States would undoubtedly encounter obstacles to the development of commercial ties. Competition would be met from Great Britain, Russia, and Japan. Of the three, Britain and Russia would be the least troublesome. Both powers seemed willing to compete in an open market for a share of China's trade. Japan, however, provided less cause for optimism. Japan had modernized rapidly; her leaders were intent upon transforming the country into a world power. A first step would likely be an effort to monopolize the economic resources of East Asia. Thus Japan would present the United States with a prime diplomatic problem: how could commercial opportunity in East Asia be maintained without antagonizing the Japanese?[11]

An indication of Foster's perception as a diplomatic observer is given in the fact that the views just summarized appeared in print before the Russo-Japanese War revealed the full extent of Japan's growing power. Tribute must also be paid to Foster as a teacher of the diplomatic arts. Later it will appear that Lansing's concept of Far Eastern problems was strikingly similar to his father-in-law's.

While Lansing lived much of his life in Washington, he remained an enigma to those who knew him there. Although he appeared frequently at formal parties and receptions and was

[11] John Watson Foster, *American Diplomacy in the Orient* (Boston and New York, 1903), pp. i, 434-437.

remembered as being invariably genial and courteous, few persons became intimately acquainted with him. The shy, diffident manner, so marked in his early years, was retained throughout his adult life and prevented him from opening his mind to casual acquaintances and professional associates. Newspaper reporters noted that he sat silently while listening to a caller. During an interview, his face would remain nearly immobile, and he sometimes made small sketches on a pad of paper. He answered questions quickly, but seldom allowed himself to be drawn into conversation. This reserve was maintained even after he became Secretary of State. Cabinet colleagues recalled that he rarely said anything at meetings unless an international question was raised. Nor did he form any close friendships with his Cabinet associates. When he was not working, his principal companions were his wife and father-in-law. The Secretary of the Navy, Josephus Daniels, probably expressed the view of many of Lansing's acquaintances in Washington when he described the man as being "capable, meticulous, metallic and mousy."[12] It is scarcely surprising that Lansing, retiring and unprepossessing, was credited by his colleagues with having little influence in the Wilson administration. Nor is it to be wondered that historians, who depended heavily on the testimony of Lansing's contemporaries, have perpetuated the idea.

What Lansing's acquaintances in Washington failed to perceive was that beneath his exterior were unobserved qualities. Lansing had a dry sense of humor, an avid interest in sports, strong religious convictions, a sense of loyalty to friends, a feeling for duty with respect to public welfare, and the tenacity to carry through projects in which he was interested. All of these traits can be seen clearly by observing Lansing's life in Watertown. After moving to Washington Lansing remarked to a cousin that he liked to return to Watertown because there "he

[12] Daniels, *Years of Peace,* p. 441. "Robert Lansing," *World's Work,* XXX (Aug., 1915), 399-400. "Our Ad-Interim Secretary," *Literary Digest,* L (June, 1915), 1545-1546.

could be himself."[13] This was an acute observation. Lansing's life in Watertown was quite different from the one he led in the capital. Many of his boyhood friends remained at home. Like Lansing, most of them were members of prominent families in town and had achieved some success in law or business. Among them Lansing dropped his reserve.[14]

Life in Watertown was relaxed and pleasant. The social group to which the Lansings belonged exchanged dinner parties. Evenings were filled with talk about books, cultural events, politics and international affairs. "Bert" and Eleanor enjoyed these affairs since both of them were well-read, cultured persons, able to converse intelligently on many subjects. The men in their early years had organized a group named "The Fortnightly Club," at first dedicated to the discussion of intellectual matters, but in later years a purely recreational organization. Every summer the members went on extended outings to Galloup Island in the St. Lawrence River during which they hiked, played baseball, pitched quoits, swam, and ate and drank well.[15] Lansing was fond of these outings. As a young man, he boxed, wrestled, and played baseball and tennis. When advancing age forced abandonment of these activities, he became an avid bass fisherman and a golfer.[16]

While living in Washington, Lansing maintained close contact with his friends. Each year he returned to Watertown to

[13] The comment was made to Mrs. John L. Gill. Interview, 1955.

[14] This point was emphasized in interviews of the author with Miss Emma Sterling Lansing and others in Watertown. Interview, 1955. Interview with the Misses Gertrude Helmer and Nama Washburn. Watertown, N. Y., June 26, 1957.

Shortly after his appointment as Secretary of State, Lansing expressed heartfelt sentiments to Gary M. Jones, Principal of the Watertown High School: "Heaven knows that I long to be with you fellows and . . . to shed the robes of state and get down to nature. . . . I want to get back to old friendships because there is nothing like the love of old friends, friends who know you and understand you."—July 1, 1915. Mrs. Seymore Jones, Watertown, N. Y., Fortnightly Club Materials. Hereinafter cited as Fortnightly Club.

[15] Fortnightly Club.

[16] Interview, 1954. *Watertown Daily Times,* Oct. 31, 1928.

spend his vacations at the home he owned there and his summer cottage at nearby Henderson Harbor on Lake Ontario. Between vacations he corresponded with his comrades.[17] This display of friendship was reciprocated. His friends never failed to arrange meetings of "The Fortnightly Club" while he was in town. Indeed, when Lansing returned from the Paris Peace Conference, the club sponsored a dinner in his honor. A highlight of the occasion was the singing of "The Old Duck Farm," one of several ditties which Lansing had composed many years earlier.[18]

Life in Watertown also had a more serious aspect. Lansing, like the President under whom he was to serve, was a devout member of the Presbyterian Church. He attended worship services regularly. For many years he was an elder of the First Presbyterian Church at Watertown, of which his brother-in-law, the Reverend Allen Macy Dulles, Sr., was pastor for a time. He taught two Sunday school classes, one for young ladies at the church and another at a church mission in an area of the city inhabited by mill workers.[19] In addition his record of community service was impressive. He served on the Library Board, Board of Education, and Safety Committee, the latter organization being aimed at the modernization of Watertown's fire and police departments.

Perhaps the most significant thing about all of the activities was the serious attention which Lansing gave to them. Although Lansing's inheritance enabled him to lead the life of a gentleman, he was no dilettante. His Sunday school work sprang from a deep interest in Biblical literature. Sometime in early life he began a critique of the Bible. Surviving records suggest that, if this criticism was not highly original, it was thorough-going. In the same manner he gave freely of himself to promote the wel-

[17] Much personal correspondence is preserved in the Library of Congress, The Papers of Robert Lansing. Hereinafter cited as Lansing Collection.

[18] *Watertown Daily Times,* Oct. 31, 1928. The club songs were printed privately under the title *The Songs of P. K.* (Watertown, 1907).

[19] Interview, 1955.

fare of the community. Lansing never missed a meeting of the Safety Committee, and he gave close attention to the most detailed aspects of its work. Local leaders attributed to Lansing much of the credit for Watertown's having one of the finest small fire companies in the country.[20] These characteristics are worth noting here because they give perspective to Lansing's State Department work. Lansing was to develop plans concerning the Far East which must have been based upon detailed studies of the records of American diplomacy and which, given the predilections of the men with whom he worked, must have been developed largely by himself. Moreover, although a distinct coolness developed between Wilson and himself, Lansing stuck with his job because he regarded resignation as tantamount to shirking his duty. In view of his record in Watertown these aspects of his official career appear to have emerged naturally from deeply ingrained work habits and character traits.

In Watertown religious and civic activities were supplemented with participation in local politics. Having decided that democracy could not survive unless citizens assumed party responsibilities, Lansing plunged into work with the Jefferson County Democrats.[21] He was for a time county chairman. In 1892 he served with his father as a delegate to the Democratic National Convention.

Virtually all of this political work was of an organizational character. Conscious that his shyness would handicap him as a candidate, he did not entertain dreams of running for office. On only one occasion was this predilection overcome. In 1902 Democratic leaders in Watertown urged him to offer himself for mayor. Normally Democratic candidates were badly beaten in city elections, but this time there was reason to think that

[20] David F. Lane, "Robert Lansing As His Friends Know Him," *Collier's Magazine,* LVI (Nov. 13, 1915), 23. Hereinafter cited as Lane, "Lansing," *Collier's.*

[21] Robert Lansing, "The Decay of American Parties," *Independent,* CXII (April 12, 1924), 193-195. Hereinafter cited as Lansing, "American Parties," *Independent.*

Lansing could win. He had won acclaim from his work with the fire department. Party leaders made a strong plea for him to enter the race. Lansing succumbed to pressure, but he proved to be a reluctant candidate. He did not wage an active campaign. His opponent, James F. Pappa, circulation manager for a local newspaper, made an aggressive canvass, especially among paper mill employees who comprised a large part of the population. Pappa talked informally with voters on the street and made speeches in which he referred to Lansing as a member of the "Finger Bowl set." These tactics enabled Pappa to overcome his initial disadvantage. He defeated Lansing by two hundred votes.[22] Several years later Lansing was urged to seek the gubernatorial nomination in New York. He flatly refused.[23] The mayoralty campaign had demonstrated that the rough-and-tumble existence of a candidate did not suit his tastes.

Lansing's political philosophy was distinctly conservative. In the 1890's he supported Grover Cleveland and opposed the reforms espoused by William Jennings Bryan. When Lansing became Secretary of State, his conservative record caused some to suspect that he did not sympathize with the "New Freedom" programs of his chief. George Creel, scarcely an admirer of the Secretary, complained that Lansing "carried conservatism to the point of medievalism."[24] This was patently an exaggeration, but there was some substance in the charge. After leaving the State Department, Lansing called publicly for the Democratic party to return to Jeffersonian principles and lashed out at "radicalism . . . masquerading as Progressivism."[25] He probably held similar views while in office,[26] but if he did, he kept them con-

[22] Interview, 1955. *Watertown Daily Times,* Oct. 31, 1928.

[23] Jacob B. Gomez to Lansing, Nov. 8, 1915; Lansing to Gomez, Nov. 10, 1915, Lansing Collection.

[24] George Creel, *Rebel at Large: Recollections of Fifty Crowded Years* (New York, 1947), p. 158.

[25] Lansing, "American Parties," *Independent,* CXIII, 193-194.

[26] Lansing to Edward M. Smith, Dec. 20, 1917, Lansing Collection. "Tendency toward Communistic Ideas," Sept. 1, 1919, Lansing Collection, "Private Memoranda."

cealed. While in the State Department, he seldom expressed to associates views on issues that did not affect his office.[27]

In short, while Lansing was a loyal Democrat, his contributions to the party were confined mostly to Jefferson County. Nor can it be said that Lansing was notably sympathetic with the ideas espoused by Wilson. These facts are significant, because they suggest that Lansing's appointments as Counselor and Secretary of State sprang from considerations which were basically non-political. Certainly such a conclusion is supported by documents bearing on his selection for the first-named of these posts.

Lansing seems to have thought of joining the State Department shortly after moving to Washington. Indeed, an attractive offer was tendered him, but he turned it down. He was, he said later, much too loyal a Democrat to receive an appointment from Republicans; however, the offer whetted his interest. Thus, when Wilson took office, Lansing sought to be designated Assistant Secretary of State. He believed that his experience especially qualified him for the work, which was concerned with protocol and departmental administration, but he soon discovered that he was pursuing a will-o'-the-wisp. The position was abolished in a departmental reorganization.[28]

Early in 1914 the office of Counselor in the State Department was left vacant by the resignation of John Bassett Moore. The Counselor served as chief legal adviser to the Secretary of State and Acting Secretary of State in the absence of the Secretary. Again Lansing was an active candidate. Among the persons he asked to recommend him for the post was Elihu Root, who was then serving as Republican Senator from New York. Root had served on a number of international commissions with Lansing. Consequently he could speak with authority about

[27] Secretary Daniels noted that Lansing "had the point of view of an old time diplomat. Never taking part in politics, he looked from afar upon the great struggles on the tariff and currency. He never went into the arena to venture all for a cause."—Daniels, *Years of Peace,* p. 441.

[28] Correspondence concerning this appointment is to be found in the Lansing Collection, I, *passim.*

Lansing's legal qualifications. Root told the President, "I have formed a very high opinion of his ability and industry. He is earnest, single-minded, and faithful to his work and has rather unusual experiences in international law."[29]

This recommendation was apparently decisive in Lansing's appointment. In the interests of political expediency, Wilson had appointed William Jennings Bryan as Secretary of State. Bryan was known to be untutored in technicalities of diplomatic intercourse. For this reason the President desired to have someone versed in international law and practice at hand to advise the Secretary. Lansing fitted these requirements. Shortly after hearing from Root, Wilson told Bryan that he was considering Lansing for the Counselorship.[30] In a few days, on March 20, 1914, Lansing entered an official service that continued until his resignation as Secretary of State six years later.

[29] Root to Wilson, March 11, 1914, Library of Congress, The Papers of Woodrow Wilson, File II, Box 48. Hereinafter cited as Wilson Papers.

[30] Wilson to Bryan, March 12, 1914, Wilson Papers, II, Letterbook. Lansing himself regarded Root's recommendation as decisive. Lansing wrote Root, "As to your personal interest in my behalf when the President had my name under consideration for Counselor, you know how deeply I feel. It was an evidence of friendship which I shall never forget."—March 4, 1915. Library of Congress, The Papers of Elihu Root, Box 51.

2. Questioning Wilson's Policy

Lansing's duties as Counselor were not entirely technical. He was often asked to propose programs for the Secretary's consideration. Some business, such as the South Manchurian freight rates dispute (an episode treated in the next chapter), was placed under his direction. On several occasions he was the Acting Secretary of State during Bryan's absences from Washington. Thus, in practice Lansing was more than the Secretary's legal adviser; he also participated in the formulation and administration of policy.

Acting in this latter broad capacity, Lansing took part in discussions concerning Japan's invasion of Shantung at the outbreak of World War I. Much of the responsibility for drafting proposals for American action as well as instructions for American diplomats devolved on him. The work provided Lansing with an opportunity to scrutinize the President's plans for East Asia. What he saw disturbed him: Wilson's policy aimed at objectives which did not accord with Lansing's concepts of American interests and, as a consequence, seemed likely to provoke trouble without benefiting the United States. This conviction prompted Lansing to seek a modification of Wilson's policy, an effort he began during the Shantung invasion and continued during most of his public career.

The main lines of Wilson's policy may be briefly described. During the first weeks of his Presidency, Wilson had been confronted with two problems involving China. One of these, the question of whether to continue official support of American members of the China Consortium, was settled by refusing to sanction the activities of the bankers. The second problem concerned diplomatic recognition of Yuan Shih-k'ai's regime. Wilson solved this by directing the American government to act independently of other nations in extending recognition. In taking these steps Wilson departed from the Taft administration's practice of co-operating with other powers in dealing with China.

Wilson's purpose was clear. He hoped that China would develop along modern, democratic, and Christian lines. Moreover, he was convinced that the United States was morally obligated to assist in the task. As a first step, the United States should promote China's independence and internal stability. If these were maintained, China would have the opportunity to make the desired changes. Secondly, American missionaries, merchants, and industrialists should be encouraged to work among the Chinese. The association would provide the Chinese with practical examples of American ways. By taking these steps the United States would perhaps gain an ally and a customer. Yet this was not Wilson's ultimate aim. The Chinese people existed amid conditions which did not provide for decent living. Nor did they enjoy the human liberties which Westerners prized. The United States, Wilson thought, should serve these repressed people by acting as a liberating force, helping them to achieve a better life. Subsequent decisions were to reveal that the President's desire to serve China was a foundation upon which American policy rested.

In its origin this China policy was thoroughly Wilsonian. The impulses which shaped it were closely related to those that gave form to the Progressive reforms at home. The President believed that the American government should serve as an agent for improving human life on every front. Viewed this way, Wilson's China policy was not unique. His aims in China, for example, were not dissimilar from his stated objectives in Latin America. Yet it must also be noted that in adopting his policy Wilson did not regard himself as breaking with the traditional objectives of American Far Eastern policy. As he viewed the record, the United States had historically sought to uphold China's independence and protect her from foreign encroachment. John Hay had expressed this aim in his Open Door notes, in which he affirmed that the United States was seeking to uphold the administrative and territorial integrity of China. Wilson regarded the Hay formula as expressive of his own policy. By withdrawing official support from the American Consortium group and extending diplomatic representation to the Republic, Wilson felt that he was upholding the principles embodied in the Hay doctrine; he believed that he broke precedent only in his decision to pursue these aims through independent measures rather than through co-operation with other powers.

In identifying his administration with the support of China's administrative and territorial integrity, Wilson had no thought of antagonizing Japan. In these early years he entertained no hostility toward the Japanese. Indeed, his handling of the California land tenure controversy revealed his desire to accord just treatment to that nation. Nevertheless, previous American support of China's integrity had encountered Japanese opposition. This had been especially true when the Taft administration had sought to implement the principle by attempting to secure the construction of an American railway in South Manchuria where the Japanese claimed exclusive investment privileges. Since Japan's interest in China was growing, she would presumably resist any efforts which would limit her future there.

An indication of trouble for the United States was forthcoming a few days after the outbreak of World War I. China, suspecting that Japan was preparing to go to war with Germany and to attack the German leasehold in Shantung, appealed for American aid. Secretary Bryan promised assistance, presumably because the threatened Japanese invasion would violate China's integrity. During the first two weeks of August, 1914, the State Department sounded the belligerents in an effort to find a formula which would exempt China from the fighting. By so doing, the Wilson administration took its first steps in opposing Japanese ambitions.

For the State Department the initial problem was to devise a suitable neutralization plan. Bryan favored an agreement neutralizing the entire Pacific area, but Lansing opposed the plan on grounds that it was impractical. British forces were reported nearly ready to move against Germany's Pacific possessions. The Peking Diplomatic Corps had already discussed a broad neutralization scheme and had discovered general opposition to any plan which included foreign military bases in the neutralization of China.[1] From this information Lansing deduced correctly that a decision had already been made to extend hostilities to the Far East. Thus, Bryan's scheme was unlikely to win approval. On August 7 Lansing handed to the Secretary a plan of his own which included an outline of proposed action and an analysis of what the United States should be trying to achieve.

The United States, Lansing said, should direct its attention to the protection of American property. The holdings of private individuals were estimated to be worth at least $42,000,000, to which figure should be added the value of property owned by the American government.[2] To avert danger of loss resulting from belligerent action, the United States should seek two agreements. One would provide for the neutralization of all Chinese territory except those places where foreign military bases were located. The second, to which all powers having an interest in

[1] John V. A. MacMurray to Bryan, July 31, Aug. 3, 1914; Josephus Daniels to Bryan, Aug. 4, 1914, National Archives, State Department Archives, file numbers 763.72/26; 763.741/3, 4; 763.72/214. Hereinafter cited as SD. MacMurray to Bryan, Aug. 6, 1914, United States Department of State, *Papers Relating to the Foreign Relations of the United States, 1914, Supplement* (Washington, 1928), p. 162. This series of documents will hereinafter be cited as *For. Rels.*

[2] C. F. Remer, *Foreign Investments in China* (New York, 1933), p. 333.

China would be parties, would provide for the maintenance of the status quo in all foreign rights and interests in China until the end of the war.

In recommending adoption of this plan, Lansing noted two additional advantages. It would, if accepted, provide safeguards for China. Furthermore, the limitations on the scope of its application might make it acceptable to the belligerents. On this latter point Lansing told Bryan:

I believe that it is possible to obtain the foregoing agreements. . . . To ask for more would, I believe, endanger all and would in any event, so delay an international arrangement as to seriously impair its value when obtained. Furthermore, to ask an agreement of a government, though not convinced that it would be granted, would accomplish no good and give an impression that this government was impractical.[3]

Bryan submitted Lansing's recommendation and his own proposal to Wilson on August 8, but no immediate action was taken on them. Mrs. Wilson had died. The grieving President did not see the papers until the fifteenth. In the meantime the arrival of information indicating Japan's definite intention of entering the war caused Lansing to revise his earlier recommendation.[4] He explained his changed view in a lengthy memorandum dated August 15.

Japan's entry into the war, Lansing pointed out, increased prospects for the intensification of the American-Japanese rivalry over China. The conflict would have its basis in the competition of Americans and Japanese for China's market. The professed interest of the Chinese in modernizing their country had caused China to be viewed widely as a rich field for foreign investments. In order to modernize, China would need huge quantities of foreign capital, supplies, and technical assistance.

[3] Lansing Memorandum, Aug. 7, 1914, United States Department of State, *Papers Relating to the Foreign Relations of the United States: The Lansing Papers, 1914-1920* (Washington, 1939-1940), I, 1-3. Hereinafter cited as *Lansing Papers* to distinguish them from the Lansing Collection.

[4] Daniels to Bryan, SD 763.72/363. Lansing to Bryan, Aug. 14, 1914; Wilson to Bryan, Aug. 17, 1914, *Lansing Papers,* I, 3-5.

While these things could probably not be supplied as long as the war lasted, alert governments would seek openings so that their citizens might benefit from China's requirements when peace was restored. In all likelihood the United States and Japan would be the primary contenders for opportunities. Europeans, who had dominated the China trade, would not play a prominent role, for European resources would be needed at home to rebuild devastated facilities. Neither the United States nor Japan, however, was likely to suffer damage from the war. Indeed, they would emerge after the war with strengthened economies. In 1914 America and Japan were debtor nations, importers rather than exporters of capital, but as a result of wartime developments, industries would be expanded and financiers would accumulate funds for investment abroad.

In competing for the China market each country had advantages. Japan's were proximity to China and an aptitude for doing business with other Orientals. America had vast financial and technical resources. These resources would provide Americans with a good chance of capturing a large part of China's business if they acted with energy. Only one barrier separated Americans from rich opportunities in China: this was the extension of Japanese hegemony over the country. Japan had recently annexed Korea and enlarged her interests in South Manchuria, where she claimed "special interests." Foreign investment capital was excluded from both of these areas. These precedents suggested that a primary American aim should be the containment of Japan's claims to exclusive privilege.

For the moment there was nothing that the United States needed to do to achieve this purpose. France, Great Britain, Germany, and Russia all claimed spheres of influence in designated areas of China. Since 1898 the powers had zealously prohibited foreigners from seeking investment opportunities in their spheres. At the end of the war the victorious powers would undoubtedly enlarge their spheres at the expense of their opponents. Japan might profit from the fight by obtaining title to German claims in Shantung, but beyond that her gains would not be extensive. However the war came out, European nations would continue to control spheres of influence which covered the major part of China.

Such a prospect, Lansing concluded, was favorable to the development of American interests. In the postwar era Britain, France, and Russia would probably alter their policy of excluding foreign investors from their spheres. Unable to supply China with capital or manufactured commodities themselves, they would be compelled by Chinese demands to provide openings for American or Japanese interests. It would be the Americans rather than the Japanese who would be admitted through this new open door. The record showed that the United States had no political aspirations in China and that Japan had definite aspirations. The best plan for the moment was to keep silent and remain watchful. Having decided on war, Japan was unlikely to assent even to limited neutralization of China. In the circumstances a proposal by the United States "would be impolitic, as rejection would weaken its influence in the future and impair its prestige."[5]

These recommendations are significant because they indicate the direction in which Lansing's thought was moving. The recommendations did not affect any immediate decisions. About the time Lansing was completing his memorandum, Wilson directed that the neutralization project be dropped. News of Japan's ultimatum to Germany led the President to the same conclusion that Lansing had reached.[6] Since these instructions eliminated the need for further discussion, Lansing placed his memorandum in his files without showing it to his superiors; however, the ideas incorporated in the document were not discarded. Lansing had again emphasized the importance of American commercial interests in China and the need for directing American diplomacy toward the safeguarding of those interests.

[5] Lansing Memorandum, Aug. 15, 1914, SD 763.72111/54 1/2.
[6] Wilson to Bryan, Aug. 17, 1914, *Lansing Papers,* I, 5.

These ideas were to become guiding principles in his handling of Far Eastern affairs.

Wilson's decision to abandon the neutralization project did not terminate consideration of China's status. As soon as it became clear that the powers would not reach an agreement, the Peking government began a new campaign. The United States was to be persuaded to protect China from military operations launched by Japan. The opening rounds of this new effort took the form of talks in the American Legation in Peking. The content of these talks and the State Department's reaction to them shed additional light on Lansing's concept of America's duty to China.

On August 19 the United States sent a sharply worded note to Tokyo reminding Japan of her pledge to consult with the United States on events which might impair China's integrity. The note was prompted by rumors that Japan was secretly supplying aid to Chinese rebels who were to stage a revolt at the same time the Japanese sent troops into Shantung.[7] Since the result might be the establishment of a pro-Japanese regime in Peking, Secretary Bryan decided to register disapproval in Tokyo. The United States, the Secretary said, was acting on the basis of the pledges of the Root-Takahira notes of 1908.[8]

The American note was transmitted officially only to Tokyo, but word of its content reached Chinese officials. On August 27, four days after Japan had declared war, Dr. V. K. Wellington Koo of the Foreign Office called upon the American Chargé d' Affaires, John V. A. MacMurray, to request a copy of the note and to discuss its meaning. In the conversation Koo intimated strongly that the Root-Takahira notes established in favor of the United States a right to be consulted with respect to any action contemplated by Japan in China's territory. For example, Japan would need America's approval before landing troops in Shantung. This suggestion was echoed by a stream of Chinese officials

[7] MacMurray to Bryan, Aug. 13, 1914, *For. Rels., 1914, Supp.*, p. 169. George Guthrie to Bryan, Aug. 15, 1914, SD 763.72/434.

[8] Bryan to Guthrie, *For. Rels., 1914, Supp.*, p. 172.

who called at the Legation during the next three weeks. Indeed, some of the callers expanded on the idea and urged that American forces in China be used to stop the invasion of Shantung by Japanese forces.[9]

MacMurray stood firm against these entreaties. The Root-Takahira exchange, he explained, was sometimes referred to as an agreement, but it was in fact simply a joint declaration of policy which did not establish a legal status. Moreover, these notes referred to only the appearance of internal disturbances in China. They made no reference to the invasion of that country. In a word, the United States was under no obligation to defend China.

These stated reasons were not the only considerations that prevented MacMurray from assenting to the Chinese pleas. The Chargé went to the heart of the matter in a dispatch which traveled by mail to Washington. American troops and naval units had been located in China to protect American life and property. It would be foolhardy to deploy these forces in defense of China. They were few in number and inadequately equipped. Their resistance would be ineffective, and the result would be war between the United States and Japan. Thus, however much the United States might regret the invasion of Shantung, there was nothing to be done to prevent it unless large forces were sent to fight Japan.

On one matter only did MacMurray recommend American action. With the outbreak of war European nations had withdrawn most of their guards from China. American forces had assumed increased responsibility. For this reason it was desirable to bring all units up to full strength. However, the United States should use caution in dispatching these forces. Japan was alerted for any indication of American aid to China. Should the Japanese mistakenly assume that American reinforcements were to be used against them, they would undoubtedly flood China

[9] MacMurray to Bryan, Sept. 10, 1914, *For. Rels., 1914, Supp.*, pp. 186-187.

with their own troops. These forces would convert China into a Japanese puppet.[10]

While MacMurray's dispatch was in transit, the American Minister to China, Paul S. Reinsch, returned to Peking. The Minister's presence effected a change in atmosphere at the Legation. Reinsch had been chosen for his post largely because he shared the President's sympathy for China. Like Wilson, he deemed it America's duty to assist with China's development. These ideas had won for the Minister great popularity among Chinese officials. As soon as the Minister re-established himself at the Legation, the Peking government renewed its campaign to enlist American support against Japan. Reinsch was approached by the Minister of Communications, who talked of Japanese plans to use Shantung as a starting point for an advance into the interior of China. Reinsch listened sympathetically and cabled a report of the conversation to Washington.[11]

Reinsch's cable and MacMurray's dispatch were read about the same time. The messages indicated that China was seeking to use the United States as an instrument of her own policy. Furthermore, Reinsch was suspected of encouraging the Chinese to believe that they might achieve their purpose. In the absence of Bryan, who was in Nebraska working for the election of Democrats to Congress, Lansing, then Acting Secretary of State, moved to set the record straight. A full statement of the aims of American policy was prepared under his direction.[12] This went forward to Reinsch on November 4.

These November 4 Instructions referred first to the protection of American life and property in China. To safeguard these interests against dangers from belligerent attack, the United States would renew its attempt to obtain an agreement neutralizing China.[13] Protection against internal disturbances would

[10] MacMurray to Bryan, Sept. 10, 1914, *For. Rels., 1914, Supp.*, p. 187.

[11] Reinsch to Bryan, Oct. 2, 1914, *For. Rels., 1914, Supp.*, p. 183.

[12] Lansing to Bryan, Nov. 2, 1914, Lansing Collection. Lansing to Edward T. Williams, Oct. 29, 1914, SD 763.72111/490.

[13] Nothing was done on this point. Tsingtao fell on November 7. The end of hostilities in China eliminated the need for an agreement.

be assured by bringing all American units up to full strength. The movement of reinforcements, the Legation was told, would be executed in a manner that would not alarm Japan.[14] The department was cognizant of Japan's anxiety and would exercise care to avoid exciting her suspicions.[15] The Instructions then commented on the requests for military assistance. MacMurray had interpreted correctly the reference to the Root-Takahira exchange in the August 19 note to Japan. The United States had registered disapproval of any activities that might lead to revolution in China. The reference was not intended to be a warning against the violation of China's neutrality. Finally, the Instructions discussed the apparent attitudes and expectations of the Peking regime. Certain Chinese officials regarded the United States as committed to defend China against foreign encroachment. This assumption had no foundation in fact. America's primary aim was "to safeguard all American rights in China, to protect all legitimate American interests there and promote by all proper methods the development of American trade." The United States was also desirous of protecting China from foreign encroachment. In promoting this latter aim the United States would exhaust all peaceful means at its disposal, but China must realize "that it would be quixotic in the extreme to allow the question of China's territorial integrity to involve the United States in international difficulties."[16]

Three days after the November 4 Instructions were sent to Peking the German garrison at Tsingtao capitulated to Japan. The surrender marked the end of hostilities on Chinese soil.

[14] Arrangements for reinforcing the China units were completed before the November 4 Instructions were sent. Lansing to Daniels (same to the Secretary of War), Oct. 3, 1914; Daniels to Lansing, Oct. 5, 1914; Secretary of War to Bryan, Oct. 6, 1914, SD 893.00/2189, 2191, 2193.

[15] Evidence of Japan's suspicions came from the press and regular departmental dispatches. "Japan's Fear of a Chino-American Entente," *Literary Digest,* XLIX (July 25, 1914), 144. MacMurray to Bryan, Aug. 13; Williams Memorandum, Aug. 13; Guthrie to Bryan, Aug. 14; MacMurray to Bryan, Aug. 18, 1914, SD 763.72/354, 1398, 812; 893.00/2184.

[16] Lansing to Reinsch, *For. Rels., 1914, Supp.,* pp. 189-190.

Chinese efforts to bring the United States to the defense of her neutrality were terminated.

For China the neutralization episode provided the first of several grave disappointments in her dealings with the United States. In withdrawing from the Consortium and extending recognition to the Chinese Republic, Wilson had indicated publicly that his administration was interested in China's welfare. The result was the hasty assumption in Peking that the United States had assumed specific obligations. America's response to China's requests for assistance provided evidence that the assumption was grounded more on hope than fact.

Viewed from the American side, the neutralization episode had another significant aspect. It revealed a division in the Wilson administration over the aims of American policy. The memoranda dated August 7 and 15 and the Instructions of November 4 set forth Lansing's firm belief that American diplomacy should be directed toward the protection of life and property in China and expansion of commercial opportunity there. He differed from Wilson and Bryan, who were primarily concerned with China's welfare. This is not to say that this latter aim was of no concern to Lansing. The November 4 Instructions express his desire to prevent foreign encroachment on Chinese territory. However, this was a secondary objective in his view. He was emphatic that the question of China's territorial integrity was not to involve the United States in "international difficulties."

Lansing's stress on commercial objectives reflected his desire to swing the Wilson policy to traditional lines. Since the opening of official treaty relations with China in 1844, the protection and enlargement of American commercial interests had been a constant objective of the United States. In contrast, the United States had vacillated in its support of China's territorial integrity. For example, Secretary of State John Hay, the very man who dispatched notes asking the powers to maintain China's territorial and administrative integrity, endeavored to obtain for the

United States a naval base and territorial concession at Samsah Bay on the coast of Fukien Province. Even Hay regarded the protection of China's integrity as being of less concern to the United States than the advancement of commercial interests. Clearly Lansing was not far from Hay in his thinking.

Lansing probably did not originate these criticisms of Wilson's policy. The fine hand of John W. Foster can be detected throughout the neutralization episode. As we have seen, the old diplomat attached great value to American commercial interests in China and worried about the effect of Japanese expansion on those interests. Diplomats, he believed, must develop a formula for accommodating American and Japanese interests. In urging less emphasis on China's integrity, Lansing was moving in the direction indicated by Foster. America's support of that principle had been one of the main sources of difficulty with Japan.

In retrospect it is evident that the neutralization episode had a significant effect on Lansing. It set him to thinking about American-Japanese problems and the means for solving them. In March, 1915, he was to offer a solution. Before turning to that story, however, we must examine another chapter in America's dealings with Japan: the South Manchurian Railway dispute. Lansing's handling of this problem also had a bearing on his proposed bargain with Japan.

3. New Light On An Old Policy

Differences between Lansing and Wilson extended beyond their views on American aims. The Counselor also questioned Wilson's concept of the Open Door policy. As has been noted, Wilson identified the Open Door with the preservation of China's administrative and territorial integrity, a broad interpretation which was based on precedents extending to Secretary Hay's notes. Lansing, in his handling of a controversy over freight rates on the South Manchurian Railway, developed another definition of the Open Door, one which was significant because it was more limited than Wilson's and was also based on precedent. Since Lansing was to base important policy recommendations on his limited concept, the story of the freight rates controversy has a place in this study.

In 1914 the State Department received complaints that the Japanese were manipulating freight rates schedules on the South Manchurian lines for the purpose of destroying the American cotton-piece-goods trade. Between 1896 and 1905 about two hundred million yards of material were sold annually. By 1914 Japanese competition had cut the total to between two and three million yards.[1] American merchants believed that the Japanese had made an official decision to drive them out of the Manchurian market.

[1] Howard Ayers, "Reviving the Cotton-Piece-Goods Trade with China," *Asia,* XVII (May, 1917), 219.

The freight rates adjustments, which were announced in June, 1914, deprived American merchandise of a price advantage that was obtained from a short haul. Customarily American goods were sent to Shanghai, reconsigned to Chinese merchants at Newchwang, Manchuria, and moved by rail from that port into the interior. Most Japanese merchants used Dairen and Antung as ports of entry, both of which were farther than Newchwang from interior markets. The new rates schedule destroyed the disparity by assigning equal rates between all three ports and Mukden.[2]

Later in the controversy the State Department learned that the allegations against the Japanese were not entirely correct. The Japanese policy, which had prompted the rates changes, was not aimed at the destruction of American trade.[3] Rather, Japan was seeking the development of the Antung to Mukden route so that her ties with South Manchuria might be strengthened. Nevertheless, the destruction of American business seemed likely to be the result. Japanese manufacturers already possessed advantages arising from cheap labor, proximity to the market, and sales organizations which eliminated middlemen's profits. If the Japanese received the additional benefit of low freight rates, American goods would no longer be competitive. To avert this danger the American Vice-Consul in Dairen, George C. Hanson, recommended an American protest against the announced changes on the grounds that they violated the Open Door. This policy, he urged, "if it means anything, surely means that trade in Manchuria should be subject to legitimate competition."[4]

The State Department did not act immediately on Hanson's suggestion. Lansing, who, at the time the Vice-Consul's dispatch was received, was Acting Secretary of State, did not believe that

[2] George C. Hanson to Bryan, June 17; Adolph A. Williamson to Bryan, Oct. 9, 1914, *For. Rels., 1915* (Washington, 1924), pp. 594-595, 600.

[3] Hanson to Bryan, April 22, to Guthrie, April 29, 1914, SD 893.773/4, 5. Williamson to Guthrie, July 24, 1916, SD 793.94/517.

[4] To Bryan, June 17, 1914, *For. Rels., 1915*, pp. 594-595.

it would be wise to press the matter. In part this decision rested on a view of the Open Door which differed from the one advanced by the Vice-Consul. To understand this view, it will be necessary to review the content of Secretary Hay's notes and the pledges made in response to them.

During the closing years of the nineteenth century, the great European powers had established spheres of influence in China. These spheres ushered in an era of special privilege in designated regions. Although the United States professed not to recognize the spheres, she was obliged to regard them as accomplished facts. The purpose of the Hay note of 1899, therefore, was merely to preserve such equality of commercial and industrial opportunity as had not been already destroyed. To do this Hay asked the powers to agree to three specific things. Within their spheres they were (1) not to interfere with any existing treaty port or vested interest, (2) to apply the Chinese treaty tariff to all imported or exported merchandise, and (3) to levy non-discriminatory harbor dues and transportation fees on all merchandise. The powers gave only conditional assent to these proposals.

Subsequent to the dispatch of the first Hay notes, the United States attempted to obtain international acceptance of a broader definition of the Open Door embodying all principles on which equal commercial and industrial opportunity in the Far East may be said to have depended, such as, for example, the integrity and administrative entity of China. The powers responded to the American prodding by affirming their support for the Open Door, but these declarations seemed meaningless. There was no abatement of claims to "special privilege" in China. Indeed, as has been noted, Secretary Hay himself sought special concessions. Thus the Open Door continued to be a limited and somewhat vague doctrine until it was redefined at the Washington Conference in 1922. The complaints against the South Manchurian Railway arose at a time when European powers and Japan claimed spheres of influence in China and were applying in them at best only the limited Open Door requested by Hay in 1899.

Lansing recognized that the nebulous state of the Open Door reduced America's chance for obtaining redress in the freight rates controversy. Writing to MacMurray, he said:

> The formal and repeated adherences on the part of the powers to the principles of equality of commercial opportunity in China are constantly being disregarded by Russia and Japan in Manchuria without protest on the part of the other powers concerned and thus can be said to be of no practical effect.[5]

It was probably true, Lansing continued, that the announced rate changes violated the spirit of the Open Door doctrine, but these changes were not an infringement of the letter of the Hay note of 1899. An American representation should rest on this latter note, rather than on vague professions of support for the principle of equal opportunity.[6]

While this was sufficient reason for withholding an American protest, Lansing saw still another flaw in the suggested action. The amount of trade with Manchuria was small. If the United States asked concessions for this trade, Japan might be provoked into reopening the entire California land tenure question which had been so troublesome in the past. This prospect made it doubtful whether a protest would be expedient.[7]

Lansing's decision ended discussion until October, 1914. At that time new information caused the matter to be reopened. A third change was made in rates schedules. All merchandise consigned by shippers to buyers in Mukden or more northerly points was to be given a 30 per cent reduction in rates on the

[5] July 30, 1914, SD 893.773/9. In a letter addressed to Senator Theodore E. Burton, Lansing expressed his opinion more cautiously: "The policy of those countries with respect to the principle of equality of opportunity in China which have repeatedly been declared to be in conformity with that of the United States, has in some instances, the Department has reason to believe, been modified to meet changing circumstances."—April 20, 1914, SD 893.773/1.

[6] Lansing to MacMurray, July 30; Aug. 17, 1914, SD 893.773/9, 13.

[7] Lansing to MacMurray, July 30, 1914, SD 893.773/9.

South Manchurian Railway provided the merchandise was delivered to coastal terminals in Japanese ships.[8] This seemed to be a direct violation of the Japanese pledge to levy no higher harbor dues or transportation charges on foreign merchandise traveling through its sphere than on merchandise belonging to its own nationals.[9] The dispatches telling of this move followed earlier ones describing a British protest against the change in freight rates. The Japanese response had been conciliatory.[10] These developments answered earlier objections to an American protest. Sometime during the first part of November, Lansing, again the Acting Secretary of State, decided that circumstances permitted an American protest. One was prepared and went forward on November 19.

Objection was made to all three of the rate changes announced by Japan. These changes, it was contended, violated Japan's repeated pledges to support the principle of equal opportunity, especially the pledge contained in Japan's reply to the Hay note of 1899. The changes infringed upon the pledge contained in the same note not to discriminate against foreign goods in the matter of freight rates and navigation privileges. Finally, the changes contravened the understanding expressed in the Root-Takahira notes that the United States and Japan would encourage the free development of commerce and industry by all nations in China.[11]

Japan responded by opening talks which resulted in concessions to the American view. Late in January, 1915, Japan agreed to extend the 30 per cent reduction in rates to all goods consigned to Mukden or points north regardless of the nationality of the carrying vessel.[12] Previously the State Department had learned that the Japanese Foreign Minister had assured the British Ambassador that goods from any foreign port would

[8] Albert W. Pontius to Bryan, Oct. 3, 1914, *For. Rels.*, 1915, pp. 598-599.
[9] Reinsch to Bryan, Oct. 28, 1914, *For. Rels., 1915,* pp. 603-604.
[10] Guthrie to Bryan, July 4; Oct. 8, 1914, *For. Rels., 1915,* pp. 598, 600.
[11] Lansing to Guthrie, *For. Rels., 1915,* pp. 606-607.
[12] Hanson to Bryan, Jan. 28, 1915, *For. Rels., 1915,* p. 612.

be accorded the same rates as goods shipped from or through Japan.[13]

On the remaining points Japan denied that the United States had valid grounds for protest. No discriminatory treatment was involved in equalizing the rates between Mukden and the three seaport terminals. The same rates applied to foreigners and Japanese. This argument also applied to another complaint raised during the conversations by the American Ambassador, George Guthrie. Guthrie contended that the failure to accord a rates reduction to goods shipped to points south of Mukden constituted a discriminatory practice. The Japanese replied that the practice was applied uniformly to all shippers. Indeed, some Japanese businessmen had complained bitterly about the latter practice, but the railway had refused any adjustment.[14]

Thus by the end of March, 1915, Japan had acceded to two stipulations of the American protest: first, the route of shipment, and, second, the nationality of the carrying vessel were not to be made the basis of discriminatory rates. Presumably Japan made these changes because the announced schedules violated pledges made in response to the first Hay note. With regard to the other points raised by the United States, Japan recognized no legal obligation to make the suggested alterations. At this point in the controversy the pressure of business resulting from the Twenty-one Demands prompted a temporary suspension of the exchanges on freight rates. When the exchanges were resumed, the United States was to inject a new element into the controversy. The purpose of this action will be discussed presently.

Before turning to other matters, however, a word about the significance of the freight rates controversy is in order. From the correspondence reviewed it is evident that Lansing recognized the existence of two definitions of the Open Door. The powers had repeatedly declared their support of the principles

[13] Guthrie to Bryan, Oct. 8, 1914, *For. Rels., 1915,* p. 600.
[14] Guthrie to Bryan, March 29, 1915, *For. Rels., 1915,* p. 616.

of equal opportunity and China's integrity, but they had neither made firm commitments to uphold these principles, nor defined what they understood them to mean. The responses to the first Hay notes were as close as the powers had come to obligating themselves in the name of the Open Door. Lansing believed that these were important facts to keep in mind. He had no objection to the American government's pressing for acceptance of a broad definition of the Open Door. In fact he was to use the broadest construction of the doctrine as an instrument of his own diplomacy on several occasions. What American officials should remember, he thought, was that a broad construction of the Open Door was not an internationally accepted formula which could be applied to the settlement of conflicts in China. Recognition of these limitations prompted Lansing to respond cautiously to recommendations that the Open Door be applied to the freight rates controversy. He advised similar restraint when Bryan and Wilson proposed to use the doctrine to combat the implementation of Japan's Twenty-one Demands.

4. A Proposed Bargain With Japan

The Twenty-one Demands crisis of 1915 was the occasion on which Wilson and Lansing's differing concepts made the first major impact on American diplomacy. Before the crisis Wilson had not appeared to regard his support of China's administrative and territorial integrity as setting the United States in opposition to Japan. The Sino-Japanese negotiations, however, persuaded the President that Japan posed the greatest threat to China's integrity. Thus, by April, 1915, a determination to prevent the expansion of Japanese interests in China had become a part of Wilson's Far Eastern policy. Lansing, on the other hand, reacted in another way. The Counselor's doubts about America's moral duty to China and his recognition that other powers had failed to accept America's definition of the Open Door doctrine caused him to question whether the Japanese demands should involve the United States in controversy. Indeed, fearful that an American-Japanese rivalry might limit American opportunity in East Asia, Lansing proposed that the United States attempt to settle its differences with Japan. For a few weeks Lansing's idea was incorporated into American diplomacy, only to be dropped when Wilson withdrew his support from the plan. Two years later, in the spring of 1917, Lansing was to try once again to win Wilson's approval of his idea. Thus, Lansing's activities during the Twenty-one Demands crisis are important not only because they contribute to an understanding of that episode, but also because they form part of the background from which the Lansing-Ishii talks were to emerge.

Lansing's concern over the Twenty-one Demands stemmed from his fears for the safety of American interests in China. Between the outbreak of war and March, 1915, China was repeatedly threatened by Japan. Following the capitulation of German forces in Shantung, Japan indicated that she would occupy key points in the province. No clear assurances were given concerning the ultimate disposition of the areas that were seized.[1] The Twenty-one Demands, if granted, would provide Japan with a legal basis for claiming exclusive privileges in vast regions of China. Neither of these steps, as far as the State Department knew, was opposed by Europe. Expediency seemed to dictate that the belligerents not oppose Japan.[2] These considerations caused Lansing to doubt the soundness of an earlier assumption. He was no longer certain that American interests would automatically be protected. If these interests were to be preserved, the United States must act on its own behalf. A basic step would be an understanding with Japan.

An opportunity to present an outline of such an understanding to the Secretary of State occurred late in February. Having received from Japan an incomplete list of her demands, Bryan decided to express formally the American view. After consulting with Wilson, he drafted the framework of a note in which opposition was stated to certain provisions of Group V. These provisions, Bryan asserted, violated Japanese pledges to maintain China's territorial and administrative integrity.[3] However,

[1] Reinsch to Bryan, Nov. 25; Dec. 24, 1914, SD 893.00/2238;763.72/1418. Guthrie to Bryan, Dec. 12, 1914, *For. Rels., 1914, Supp.*, p. 206.

[2] Bryan to Walter Hines Page; Page to Bryan, August 11, 1914, *For. Rels., 1914, Supp.*, pp. 165-167. Bryan to Page, Feb. 2; Page to Bryan, Feb. 13, 1915, *For. Rels., 1915* (Washington, 1924), pp. 82, 88.

[3] Bryan to Wilson, Feb. 22, 1915, The National Archives, The Correspondence of William Jennings Bryan and Woodrow Wilson. Hereinafter cited as Bryan-Wilson Cor. Wilson to Bryan, February 25, 1915, *Lansing Papers,* II, 407.

Lansing objected to the plan. He felt that Japan's commitment to uphold China's integrity was insufficiently precise to make that principle the sole basis of a protest. Moreover, Bryan was mistaken in his decision to confine the proposed note to a single group of the demands. There were other provisions which seemed equally objectionable.

On February 26 and March 1, Williams, who appears to have acted at Lansing's instigation, and Lansing sent Bryan detailed suggestions.[4] To confine American views to Group V alone, they advised, would create the impression that the United States had no objection to the remaining demands. Such an interpretation would be unfortunate. In Group II Japan requested a legal status which would give her the right to exclude foreign interests from South Manchuria and Eastern Inner Mongolia. The provisions for exclusive mining and iron manufacturing rights in Group III would have the effect of barring American capital from a large area in central China, a development which would violate provisions in Sino-American treaties stipulating that any right, privilege, or favor granted by China to any nation would also accrue to the United States.[5] Should the United States allow its treaty rights to be violated without obtaining concessions in return, a precedent would be established. The same procedure might be applied by Japan in Shantung and Fukien provinces; France, in Yunnan; Britain,

[4] The factual content of the memorandum which went to Bryan over E. T. Williams' signature was undoubtedly brought together by the Chief of the Far Eastern Division, but the policy recommendations based on it were Lansing's. The Desk Diary in the Lansing Collection shows almost daily conferences between Williams and Lansing. While no record of these talks exists, Lansing probably used them to persuade Williams to join him in making recommendations to Bryan. Williams had expressed no previous interest in making such a deal with Japan. Nor did he return to the idea at a later time. Indeed, Williams' record in the State Department is notable chiefly because he was one of the most outspoken opponents of any steps which could be construed as infringements on China's integrity.

[5] The specific articles were as follows: Treaty of 1844, XV; 1858, XXX; 1868, VIII; and 1903, III, VII. The texts are printed in China, The Imperial Maritime Customs, *Treaties, Conventions, Etc., between China and Foreign States* (2nd ed., New York, 1921), I, 677, 729, 953.

in central China; and Russia, in North Manchuria and Mongolia. China, in effect, would be irrevocably closed to American businessmen, educators, and missionaries.

At the same time, there were good reasons for making concessions to Japan. The most important of these was America's inability to take any practical steps to force Japan from some of the positions she held. Groups I and II were simply requests for legal recognition of privileges already assumed in large measure by Japan in Shantung and South Manchuria. Armed force would probably be required to oust Japan from these regions. Americans might entertain the deepest sympathy for China, but they were not prepared to support an armed defense of her integrity.

Not only would an attempt to stand firm against these demands be futile, but the effort might result in harm. MacMurray's warning about Japanese troops flooding China continued to haunt Lansing. With Japanese national pride inflated by quick victories over German forces, Japan could not be counted on to impose reasonable restraints on herself. Unyielding American opposition to her national aspirations might yet cause her to embark upon a venture to control China.

Finally, the United States must consider Japan's economic and strategic interests. South Manchuria and Eastern Inner Mongolia were sparsely inhabited areas which might serve as outlets for Japan's rapidly expanding population. Shantung and South Manchuria contained valuable raw materials for an industrial nation. Moreover, these latter territories were adjacent to the Japanese islands. Japan could ill afford to have them controlled by hostile powers. In pursuing its own safety, the United States did not permit any power to challenge its hegemony in the Caribbean Sea. As a matter of equity, America should not object to other nations' advancing similar claims.

All of these considerations suggested a bargain along the following lines. The United States would recognize formally that Japan had "special interests" in South Manchuria, Eastern Inner

Mongolia, and Shantung. In return Japan would (1) agree to make no further complaint with regard to alien land legislation in the United States unless the legislation was confiscatory in nature or affected vested rights; (2) reaffirm the principle of the Open Door, making it particularly applicable to the areas in China where Japan possessed "special interests"; and (3) prevent any monopolization by Japanese subjects of particular trades in these areas and any preferential rates or treatment by Japanese transportation concerns for the benefit of Japanese subjects or their merchandise.

The United States would obtain two advantages from the proposed bargain. One would be the settlement of the troublesome alien land question. In 1913 Japan had protested strongly against California legislation barring aliens "ineligible for citizenship" from holding agricultural land. Tokyo had asked nullification of the law on grounds that it violated the American-Japanese Treaty of 1911. The Wilson administration had denied any infringement of Japanese treaty rights, but the President, seriously disquieted by the legislation, had sought unsuccessfully to block passage of the bill. By early 1915 the unresolved dispute seemed destined to be reopened when the Oregon and Idaho legislatures began debating bills patterned after the California law.[6] A pledge such as Lansing suggested would prevent a repetition of an embarrassing controversy.

The second and third pledges suggested by Lansing would provide protection for American commerce inside Japanese spheres of influence. The South Manchurian freight rates controversy had demonstrated that the United States lacked legal safeguards for its commerce in areas where Japan claimed "special privileges." This was partly due to the vagueness of the Open Door itself and partly to the fact that Japan claimed no spheres at the time the Open Door notes were written. To settle the current dispute and prevent future ones, Japan should do two related things. She should redeclare her intention to main-

[6] Robert Lansing, *War Memoirs of Robert Lansing* (New York, 1935), p. 283. Hereinafter cited as Lansing, *War Memoirs.*

tain the Open Door, especially in Shantung, South Manchuria, and Eastern Inner Mongolia. Then, to make perfectly clear what was meant by her declaration, Japan would define her understanding of the doctrine. The definition suggested by Lansing was based on the pledges requested by Secretary Hay in 1899.

Japan would probably make the concessions just outlined in return for American recognition of her "special interests." In 1912 Foreign Minister Yasuya Uchida had made a similar proposal to Secretary of State Philander Knox while the latter was on a tour of Japan. More recently, on February 15, 1915, the American Ambassador, George Guthrie, had cabled that the Japanese Premier, Shigenobu Okuma, had expressed a desire to reach an understanding with the United States. According to the Premier, Japan would give certain pledges concerning the integrity of China and would be willing to extend the Anglo-Japanese alliance to include the United States. Although these ideas were expressed as carefully guarded intimations, Guthrie regarded them as indications of a genuine desire to end the growing American-Japanese rivalry.[7] Lansing concurred.[8]

Lansing discussed his proposed bargain with Bryan on March 1. While no record of the conversation was kept, the Secretary appears to have approved the idea. Bryan viewed Japanese aspirations with the same sympathy that he did those of China. A few days earlier he had suggested to the President that China might be wise to recognize Japan's claims in Manchuria, if, by so doing, she could secure guarantees against further encroachment.[9] Thus he offered no objection to the plan to recognize Japan's "special interests." He did, however, oppose spelling out American desires at that time. The Wilson administration was not agreed on the way in which the alien land question was to be resolved. Bryan and Wilson had discussed the negotiation of a

[7] Guthrie to Bryan, Feb. 15, 1915, SD 811.52/277.

[8] Williams to Bryan, Feb. 26, 1915, Library of Congress, The Papers of William Jennings Bryan. Hereinafter cited as Bryan Papers. Lansing to Bryan, March 1, 1915, *Lansing Papers,* II, 407-408.

[9] Bryan to Wilson, Feb. 22, 1915, Bryan-Wilson Cor.

treaty which would nullify conflicting state legislation, but they had decided to postpone any decision until the Twenty-one Demands crisis was settled.[10] For this reason the Secretary could not approve a definite proposal to Japan. Nor could he approve one other suggestion. The text of the demands given the American government by Japan omitted the full text of Group III. Since it was inexpedient to express an opinion of these articles without having formal knowledge of them, Lansing had recommended an inquiry.[11] But Bryan presumably feared such a move would prevent the United States' taking effective action on the demands before the Chinese-Japanese negotiations were ended. The American view must go forward quickly. With these two exceptions Bryan approved Lansing's suggestions and requested the Counselor to draft a statement.[12] When the job was done, Lansing's draft was reviewed by Williams, Bryan, and Wilson, the latter of whom commented that it was "thorough and satisfactory" and suggested only a few verbal changes. On March 13 the entire statement was cabled to Tokyo over Bryan's signature.

The March 13 Note opened with a preamble stating the grounds for American intervention in the Twenty-one Demands crisis. Should the Japanese demands become operative, certain of them would violate American treaty rights and the established principles of equal opportunity for industry and commerce and the integrity of China. In the case of the threat to the latter principles, the American government averred that it was acting in accord with terms of the Root-Takahira notes and out of a feeling of "moral obligation" to other interested powers then engaged in war.

Turning next to specific provisions, the Note called attention to Groups I and II which related to Shantung, South Man-

[10] Bryan to Wilson, Jan. 23; Wilson to Bryan, Jan. 27, 1915, Bryan Papers.

[11] Bryan to Reinsch, Feb. 24, 1915, SD 793.94/236. Williams to Bryan, Feb. 26, 1915, Bryan Papers. Lansing to Bryan, March 1, 1915, *Lansing Papers,* II, 408.

[12] Bryan to Wilson, March 6, 11, 1915, Bryan Papers.

churia, and Eastern Inner Mongolia. The requests for special and exclusive privileges in these areas violated the principles of equal opportunity and American treaty rights. However, the United States would not protest against these demands "at this time," because it "frankly recognizes that territorial contiguity creates special relations between Japan and these districts." Nor did the American government perceive "any special menace to its existing rights and interests" in the terms of Group III, which requested mining and iron manufacturing rights in central China; or in Group V, Articles 2, 5, and 7: namely, requests to establish Japanese churches, hospitals, and schools; to permit Japanese to own land in the interior of China; to grant certain railway concessions south of the Yangtze River; and to permit Buddhist missionaries to operate in China.

Exception was taken to five of the demands. Group V, Article 4, restricting China's arms and munitions purchases to Japanese manufacturers, and Article 6, contemplating a Japanese monopoly over Fukien Province, would, if they became operative, violate the principle of equal opportunity and American treaty rights. Group IV, which provided for non-alienation of the Chinese coast; Group V, Article 1, which required China to employ Japanese advisers on administrative, financial, and military affairs; and Article 3, which asked the creation of joint police forces, were regarded by the United States as objectionable because they were clearly "derogatory to the political independence and administrative entity" of China.

Finally, the Note turned to Japan's fears concerning American opposition to her aspirations. Japan was informed that the United States viewed Japanese aspirations in the Far East with "friendship and esteem." Furthermore, the American government could not too "earnestly impress upon . . . [Tokyo] that the United States is not jealous of the prominence of Japan in the East or of the intimate co-operation of China and Japan for their mutual benefit. Nor has the United States any intention of obstructing or embarrassing Japan, or influencing China in opposition to Japan." In short, the United States would not oppose Japanese aspirations as long as she did not seek to monopolize commerce and investments in China beyond the limits of her spheres of influence.[13]

The March 13 Note was a remarkable document. Its text accomplished several things. It maintained America's strongest position from which to bargain with Japan. Broad claims concerning the binding character of the pledges made by Japan to maintain China's integrity were asserted at the outset. From Lansing's earlier comments about the Open Door and Root-Takahira Notes, it is clear that he questioned the validity of the pledges to uphold China's integrity and America's legal obligation to support the principle. Nevertheless, assertion of the claim kept the record clear. The United States remained in a position to use a broad construction of the Open Door as an instrument in its diplomacy. Another feature worthy of note was the safeguard erected to protect American interests. The Note claimed the right to protest against all provisions giving Japan exclusive privilege. This claim was modified, however, by stating America's disinclination to counter Japanese aims in Shantung, South Manchuria, and Eastern Inner Mongolia "at this time," and failing to perceive "any special menace to its existing rights and interests" in the professed Japanese desires in central China. By employing such phraseology, the American government implied a willingness to make concessions without actually conceding anything. The total effect was to retain every possible advantage for the United States. The Note made no final concession to Japan's claims of exclusive privilege and abandoned none of America's diplomatic weapons. The United States remained in a position to maintain all of its rights and interests in China and full support of China's integrity. At the same time, the withholding of a protest against certain demands and expressing of profound friendship for Japan was a clear

[13] Bryan to the Japanese Ambassador, March 13, 1915, *For. Rels., 1915*, pp. 105-111.

hint of a willingness to make a deal. Certainly a document which combined all of these purposes was not the work of an amateur diplomat.

The United States and Japan began shortly to consider adjustment of certain demands. The story of these negotiations need not be told here. It will suffice to say that Japan revised, abandoned, or postponed provisions to which the United States objected. Pressure exerted by the United States appears to have been a factor, though not the only one, in achieving this result.

While this is now evident, the American government had no advance knowledge of the final Sino-Japanese terms. As late as May 6, two weeks before conclusion of negotiations in Peking, Bryan was informed by the Japanese Ambassador that Japan was continuing to press for all of the demands to which objections had been made in the American Note.[14] Japan was aware of the close communications between Washington and Peking. She did not deem it expedient to inform China of forthcoming concessions through Washington.

Japan's official silence had a significant effect on the course taken by the United States. To this point Wilson had exhibited a measure of sympathy for Japan's aspirations. He had shared the opinion that Japan as a progressive, expanding nation must be permitted opportunities for national development. He had believed that Japan could develop economic hegemony over contiguous areas of the continent without impairing China's sovereignty. But his opinion changed when he learned that Japan was apparently unwilling to follow American suggestions with respect to certain demands. He grew suspicious of Japanese intentions, apparently thinking that Japan was aiming at the seizure of China. From this time forward he opposed any Japanese move which might be construed as an infringement on China's integrity. This view was manifest in his instructions to Bryan to be "as active as the circumstances permit in showing

[14] Japanese Foreign Office to the Japanese Ambassador (copy left at the State Department); Memorandum handed the Secretary of State by the Japanese Ambassador, April 30, 1915, *For. Rels., 1915,* pp. 141, 128-130.

ourselves to be champions of the sovereign rights of China, now as always, though with no thought of seeking any special advantage for ourselves."[15] This view was shared by other key officials. From this time on Bryan, Williams, and Reinsch entertained dark suspicions concerning Japan's ultimate aims.

In the middle of April Wilson assumed personal direction of American diplomacy. To bolster Peking's resistance, China was informed that the United States had conceded nothing to Japan.[16] An effort was made to apply pressure on Tokyo by issuing a public statement declaring America's opposition to any settlement which infringed China's integrity, the principles of equal opportunity, and American treaty rights.[17] Britain, France, and Russia were urged to join the United States in representations against the demands.[18]

Japan's course was not visibly altered by these steps. Europe was unwilling to become involved in Far Eastern tangles. Britain, France, and Russia refused to make the suggested representations.[19] Without support there seemed to be nothing more the United States could do to modify the Japanese terms. On May 7, Japan demanded China's unconditional acceptance of all but Group V and threatened "necessary" measures in the event China failed to give a satisfactory response within forty-eight hours. China capitulated. Two weeks later, on May 25, China signed treaties and notes which embodied many, though by no means all, of the original objectives of the Twenty-one Demands.

While these events were taking place, Lansing developed a plan of his own. On the day Japan delivered her ultimatum to

[15] April 14, 1915, *Lansing Papers,* II, 416.

[16] Wilson to Bryan, April 14; Bryan to Reinsch, April 15, 1915, *Lansing Papers,* II, 416-417.

[17] *New York Times,* May 7, 1915. Bryan warned Japan in advance of the step. Bryan to the Japanese Ambassador, April 28, 1915, Bryan-Wilson Cor.

[18] Bryan to Page, May 6, 1915; same to Paris and St. Petersburg, *Lansing Papers,* II, 423.

[19] Page to Bryan, May 7; William Grave Sharp to Bryan, May 8; George Thomas Marye to Bryan, May 9, 1915, SD 793.94/565, 340, 343.

China, he advised the filing of a caveat with regard to the demands. Such a move would not prevent the Japanese from coercing China, but "it would constitute a complete reservation of all possible rights affecting American interests and China's interests as well, so that any agreements forced upon China at the present time could properly become the subject of discussion in the future when conditions become more propitious."[20] Lansing suggested that the American government refuse to recognize any agreement or understanding concluded by China and Japan "impairing the treaty rights of the United States and its citizens in China, or the international policy relative to China known as the open door policy."[21] Wilson, now convinced that his own measures had failed, approved the suggestion. The American reservations were sent to Japan and announced on May 11.

The May 11 caveat has generally been interpreted as evidence of the Wilson administration's stiffening attitude toward Japan. The caveat failed to reaffirm America's willingness to recognize Japanese claims in Shantung, South Manchuria, and Eastern Inner Mongolia. The omission signaled a determination to oppose the expansion of Japanese interests. This explanation suffices for Wilson, but it is less satisfactory when applied to Lansing. Lansing was not convinced that Japan's bullying of China should terminate consideration of his proposed bargain. He continued to press for acceptance of his idea until late 1917.

Lansing regarded the May 11 caveat as providing the foundation for any redress which the United States might wish to obtain from Japan. The March 13 Note was a confidential communication, which contained expressions of an American willingness to make concessions to Japan as well as of opposition to the Japanese demands. The admixture might prove embarrassing should the United States use the Note as a basis for action. The caveat, on the other hand, would provide an excel-

[20] Lansing to Bryan, May 7, 1915, *Lansing Papers,* II, 424.

[21] Bryan to Guthrie (and Reinsch), May 11, 1915, *For. Rels., 1915,* p. 146.

lent point of departure, if one were needed. Indeed, the State Department took still another step to keep the record clear with respect to the establishment of Japanese monopoly in China. On May 15 Reinsch was instructed to scrutinize the Sino-Japanese settlement for provisions affecting the status of foreign interests. The United States wished to share in any privileges won by Japan.[22]

In advising that the record be kept straight, Lansing did not abandon the idea of striking a bargain with Japan. The language of his caveat did not contradict that of his March 13 Note. The Note had not conceded American recognition of Japan's "special interests"; it had only hinted that such recognition might be extended in return for Japanese concessions. The caveat did not expunge the hint from the record, a fact which the Japanese perceived. Within a few months Tokyo was to ask the United States to affirm the phraseology of the March 13 Note. Lansing had thus kept open the possibility of a settlement of American-Japanese difficulties.

From this analysis it is clear that key members of the Wilson administration were moving along opposite paths in their thinking about Japan. Japan's threats were causing Wilson, Bryan, Reinsch, and Williams to agree on directing American diplomacy toward the protection of China's integrity. In practice this meant that the United States would oppose Japanese expansion anywhere in China. Moving in another direction was Lansing, who supported American recognition of limited Japanese expansion in return for certain Japanese pledges. It must be emphasized again that Lansing's position did not develop out of any lack of concern over China's fate. Rather, Lansing believed that there were developing in Japan pressures for the conversion of vast stretches of China into a Japanese preserve. Since American diplomacy was unlikely to block completely Japan's designs, it seemed wise to attempt to direct Japanese energies into a limited expansion program. Such tactics were likely to

[22] *For. Rels., 1915,* p. 147.

protect the largest possible measure of China's integrity, and, as a consequence, they would safeguard American interests against the danger of Japanese monopoly.

In taking this position Lansing continued his attempt to direct American policy into traditional channels. The idea of preserving American opportunity through the defense of China's integrity was rooted in nineteenth-century practice. Anson Burlingame, for example, had adopted a policy of co-operative diplomacy in order to prevent foreign encroachment from forcing Americans from China. Again, Secretary Hay admitted that his attempts to line up international support for the principle of China's integrity was inspired by a desire to protect American interests. Wilson's policy varied from these precedents by emphasizing the defense of China's integrity as an end in itself. Such a policy, Lansing believed, was inappropriate on theoretical and practical grounds. He could not agree that the United States had a moral duty to aid the Chinese. His doubts were strengthened by the prospect of deep trouble between the United States and Japan. The United States, he felt, would have the greatest success if the examples of the past were followed.

While these differences between Wilson and Lansing are clear to the historian, they were less apparent to the men themselves. Wilson does not appear to have been conscious of any disagreements with Lansing on Far Eastern questions until they went to Paris in 1919. This was not due to a lack of perception on the President's part. Rather, the failure developed from Lansing's habit of concealing his views when they varied from Wilson's. Lansing's reasons for adopting this practice is revealed by a comment on the working relationship which developed between him and the President.

Lansing, with whom psychology was a hobby, studied Wilson's personality and the ways he worked. He ascertained that Wilson would accept advice until he was ready to make a decision. When his choice was made, the President considered the matter closed and listened to no further arguments. It was unwise to urge a reversal of a decision. Wilson was unlikely to change his mind and was likely to become irritated. A change, if one were to be effected, must be sought through indirection.[23] The record suggests that Lansing was unusually adept at applying indirect pressure. His personality fitted him for such tactics. His tenacity, patience, and enormous reserve, which he had exhibited during his years in Watertown, enabled him to do that which would have been impossible for a more flamboyant spirit. He could work toward an objective while remaining quiet about what he was doing.

These observations are pertinent to the account of the Twenty-one Demands. They suggest why Wilson did not know fully Lansing's ideas on Far Eastern matters. They also suggest that in the spring of 1915 Lansing adopted new tactics to win approval of his ideas. Since Wilson was aroused against Japan, it was futile to press immediately for the proposed bargain. The President seemed certain to reject the proposal. An alternative was to say nothing and await a fresh opportunity to present the plan. As will be seen, the opportunity was to appear. Before that time, however, the relationship between Lansing and Wilson was to be transformed. A short time after China and Japan

[23] Lansing wrote several profiles of Wilson. One deserves full quotation here.

"When one comes to consider Mr. Wilson's mental processes, there is the feeling that intuition rather than reason played the chief part in the way in which he reached conclusions and judgments. In fact arguments, however soundly reasoned, did not appeal to him if they were opposed to his feeling of what was the right thing to do. Even established facts were ignored if they did not fit in with this intuitive sense, this semi-divine power to select the right. Such an attitude of mind is essentially feminine. In the case of Mr. Wilson, it explains many things in his public career, which are otherwise very perplexing.

"In the first place it gave superior place to his own judgment. With him it was a matter of conviction formed without weighing evidence and without going through the process of rational deduction. His judgments were always right in his own mind, because he knew they were right. How did he know that they were right? Why he *knew* it and that was the best reason in the world. No other was necessary."—"The Mentality of Woodrow Wilson," Nov. 20, 1921, Lansing Collection, "Private Memoranda."

terminated their discussion of the Twenty-one Demands, Lansing assumed enlarged responsibilities. On June 9, Bryan resigned as Secretary of State; two weeks later Lansing was appointed to the post.

5. The Counselor Becomes The Secretary

On June 23, 1915, Lansing, acting at the President's request, visited the Executive Offices. Wilson went directly to the purpose of the interview: Lansing was offered the post of Secretary of State. "By experience and training," the President said, "you are especially equipped to conduct the foreign affairs of the United States. This under present conditions is far more important than political influence." Furthermore, the appointment was desirable, the President said, because he and Lansing were of the "same mind concerning international policies."[1]

Lansing was surprised by the offer. He had wanted the job, but he had not expected to be appointed.[2] The President, he had assumed, would fill the post with a political appointee. However, as Lansing was to learn, Wilson was quite sincere when he said that considerations other than those of a political character guided his choice. Since these considerations were to affect Lansing's handling of Far Eastern affairs, it is important to note them here.

Lansing did not figure importantly in Wilson's initial canvass for candidates. The Counselor seemed unacceptable for two

[1] Lansing, *War Memoirs,* p. 16.

[2] Lansing's desires may be inferred from his reaction to newspaper discussion of Bryan's probable successor. The press mentioned Lansing as the most likely candidate. The opinion was based on the fact that Lansing had served frequently as Acting Secretary. In his memoirs Lansing denied instigating these speculations but did not deprecate his qualifications. Lansing's prompt acceptance of the offer also suggests that he had thought about the post for himself. Lansing, *War Memoirs,* p. 16.

reasons. His appointment would not strengthen the administration. Secretaries William C. Redfield and William G. McAdoo were from New York. A mid-westerner would facilitate the dealings of the administration with Congress.[3] Secondly, Lansing was not the kind of person Wilson wanted. At the time the President was thinking of a strong personality, a man who had ideas of his own. Lansing appeared to be lacking in this trait. "He won't oppose me," was Wilson's complaint about Lansing to Secretary of Agriculture, David F. Houston, early in June.[4] Wilson, as a result, turned to the consideration of men who were outside the State Department. Of those considered, Thomas D. Jones, a Chicago businessman, was the most attractive. As a trustee of Princeton University and loyal Democrat, Jones had supported Wilson. A year earlier Wilson had sought to reward Jones with an appointment to the newly created Federal Reserve Board, but the Senate had not confirmed his appointment. Still anxious that Jones's services should not be lost to his administration, Wilson decided to offer him the Cabinet post.[5]

The move, however, was blocked by Colonel Edward M. House. House, who was returning from his first peace mission in Europe when Bryan's resignation was announced, regarded Jones's appointment as a threat to his own position as the President's unofficial adviser on foreign affairs. Bryan had complained that his authority and prestige were damaged by House's

[3] William G. McAdoo, *Crowded Years: The Reminiscences of William G. McAdoo* (Boston and New York, 1931), pp. 238-239. Hereinafter cited as McAdoo, *Crowded Years.* The weakness of Lansing's appointment from a political standpoint was prominent in the thinking of many officials. Secretary Daniels, recalling an earlier conversation, quoted himself as saying, "I like Lansing. He is a man of ability. But he has lived in Washington most of his life. If he ever voted, nobody knows it. He brings no strength into the Cabinet."—"Memorandum by Katherine E. Brand of an Interview with Secretary Daniels," Aug. 8, 1936. Library of Congress, The Papers of Ray Stannard Baker, Series I, Box 28, Daniels File. Hereinafter cited as Baker Papers.

[4] "Memorandum by Ray Stannard Baker of an Interview with Secretary Houston," Dec. 1, 1928. Baker Papers, I, Box 37, Houston File.

[5] Edward M. House to Eleanor Foster Lansing, April 13, 1931, Yale University Library, The Papers of Edward M. House. Hereinafter cited as House Papers.

interference. Jones, House feared, might seek to destroy the arrangement. Thus, before House's ship reached its berth in New York the Colonel began to seek a change in the President's decision. Dudley Malone appeared to brief House on Wilson's plans. Secretary McAdoo, who may have been interested in the post for himself, journeyed to New York to discuss the appointment.[6] From these conferences House obtained the information that he needed: Wilson, he learned, was still open to advice. Moreover, he had discovered a suitable candidate of his own. On June 16 he gave his counsel in a letter to Wilson.

House believed that two qualities were essential in the next Secretary: he should have sufficient ability to direct State Department affairs, and he should be compliant enough to accept the joint leadership of House and Wilson. Although House did not claim to know Lansing well, the Counselor seemed to fit these specifications. Lansing's work, especially with neutrality problems, had enhanced his reputation as an international lawyer. As for the second requirement, all who knew Lansing testified that he was a most unassuming man. These qualities were presented to Wilson in the following way:

> I have a feeling that if Lansing is at all acceptable to you that [*sic*] he could be used to better advantage than a stronger man. It seems to me that the whole office should be reorganized, a very efficient man being placed as First Secretary and another as Second Secretary. These with Lansing would be able to do the details intelligently, and you could direct as heretofore and without half the annoyance and anxiety that you have been under.
>
> I think the most important thing is to get a man with not too many ideas of his own and one that will be entirely guided by you without unnecessary argument, and this, it seems to me, you would find in Lansing. I only met him once and then for a few minutes only, and while his mentality did not impress me unduly, at the same time, I hope you have found him able enough to answer the purpose indicated.[7]

[6] House Papers, The Diary of Edward M. House, June 13, 14, 16, 1915. Hereinafter cited as House Diary.

[7] June 16, 1915, Wilson Papers, II, 82.

This advice caused the idea of appointing a strong personality to fade from the President's mind. Wilson was content with his arrangements with House and did not wish to have them disturbed. In consequence, he decided to appoint Lansing. Lansing was needed, Wilson told McAdoo, to put diplomatic notes in order and to advise on questions of international law. From these remarks McAdoo understood that Wilson intended to decide on all policy matters. Lansing's function would be simply the execution of the President's decisions.[8] That this was a correct interpretation of Wilson's purpose is indicated by similar testimony from other Cabinet members.[9]

Nor were the President's motives concealed from Lansing. Wilson discussed with Lansing his plans for working with the Secretary of State before offering him the job.[10] House discussed his own position in the administration with Lansing a few weeks after the appointment was announced. During these conversations, Lansing agreed to accept the conditions that were proposed. After his talk with Lansing, House recorded, "I feel that I have a working partner in the State Department who will carry his full share."[11] Further evidence of Lansing's commitment is to be found in his performance as Secretary. With the exception of his outburst at Paris in 1919, Lansing never complained about Wilson's handling of foreign affairs. He also accepted the close relationship of Wilson and House. Indeed, he sometimes used this relationship for his own purposes. House became a channel for ideas which the President would have found unpalatable if they had come directly from the State Department.

Lansing kept in mind the circumstances of his appointment as he dealt with Far Eastern problems. Although his elevation

[8] McAdoo, *Crowded Years,* pp. 338-339.

[9] The views of Secretaries Albert S. Burleson and Daniels are in Daniels, *Years of Peace,* p. 436. Those of the Secretary of Agriculture are in David F. Houston, *Eight Years with Wilson's Cabinet, 1913 to 1920* (Garden City, 1926), I, 141.

[10] House Diary, June 24, 1915.

[11] House Diary, July 24, 1915.

to Cabinet rank gave him new prestige and power, he continued to move cautiously in pressing for acceptance of his own ideas. His experience as Counselor had revealed that he differed sharply with Wilson on crucial points. The conditions attached to his appointment indicated that Wilson would not welcome the Secretary's making policy recommendations which diverged from his ideas. Lansing's response, therefore, was not to abandon his plans but to continue to press for their adoption through the use of indirect tactics.

6. The Waiting Game

As Secretary, one of Lansing's tasks was to cope with the diverging American and Japanese aims in South Manchuria and Eastern Inner Mongolia. Japan continued to take advantage of the West's preoccupation with the war in order to strengthen the legality of her claims to "special interests" in those regions. A first step was the signing of a treaty in 1916 with Russia which placed limits on the latter's sphere of influence. Almost simultaneously China was presented with a new set of demands. Both moves sprang from a common purpose: Japan was trying to establish her claims on a basis which could not be challenged by other powers when the war ended. Wilson, on the other hand, now deeply suspicious of Japanese ambitions, directed that the United States try to block the assertion of new Japanese claims to "special interests" and to seek the elimination of Japanese monopoly wherever it existed in China.

Lansing concurred with part of the President's aims. The next chapter will show that Lansing joined Wilson in working for the end of all foreign monopoly in China Proper. The Secretary also agreed that the United States should file reservations whenever Japan claimed exclusive privileges in South Manchuria and Eastern Inner Mongolia. The reservations would enable the State Department to seek redress for the curtailment of American treaty rights, if it seemed in the future desirable to make such claims. But Lansing thought privately that it would be most unwise for the United States to indicate its intention to seek the abolition of Japan's "special interests" in these latter regions. In part his thought was prompted by considerations of expediency. The ever-deepening troubles of the United States with the European belligerents made it unwise to touch Japan's sensitive spot. Equally important was the fact that Japan had not given her reaction to the bargain outlined in the March 13 Note. Until Japan gave her views Lansing was determined to avoid steps which might lead Japan to assume that it would be futile to negotiate with the United States. Thus in directing American diplomacy Lansing took into account three points of view: Japan's, Wilson's, and his own. That it was not always easy to bridge the differences among these viewpoints is revealed by the story of controversies relating to South Manchuria and Eastern Inner Mongolia which developed between Lansing's elevation to the Cabinet and America's entry into World War I.

The first trouble was over freight rates on the South Manchurian Railway. By March, 1915, it seemed that these problems had been resolved, but a month later, amid signs that Japan intended to coerce China into accepting the entire list of the Twenty-one Demands, Japan refused to give the same reduction in freight rates to goods arriving at Newchwang in American vessels as to those arriving in Japanese vessels. The State Department, having witnessed the stiffening of Japan's attitude in the Sino-Japanese negotiations, concluded that Japan had decided to drive foreign competitors from the scene. To meet this threat a new American protest was prepared.[1]

Ambassador Guthrie was to bring to the attention of the Japanese Foreign Office the failure of the South Manchurian Railway to accord non-discriminatory treatment to American merchandise. Japan was to be asked to remedy the situation immediately. Furthermore, in making the request, Guthrie was to say that the United States suspected the Japanese of trying to squeeze American trade out of South Manchuria. For exam-

[1] Williams Memorandum, April 13, 1915, SD 793.94/292.

ple, the South Manchurian Railway's practice of extending freight rate reductions only to goods transported in Japanese vessels would result in the elimination of American goods from the market. These goods flowed into South Manchuria along the Shanghai to Newchwang route. No Japanese vessels plied this route, and American merchants, therefore, were denied an opportunity to seek relief. Japan was thus guilty of violating the principle of equal opportunity.[2]

As on past occasions, the Japanese reply was couched in conciliatory language. Renewed assurances were given of Japan's intention to accord non-discriminatory treatment to merchandise which was brought to South Manchuria in non-Japanese ships. Moreover, all merchandise would be given equal treatment in the handling of cargo and related matters. In response to the allegation about the lack of Japanese shipping between Shanghai and Newchwang, the Japanese presented a list of recent sailings which demonstrated that the United States was misinformed.[3] It was conceded, however, that there had been a delay in extending rates reductions. Differences in business practices, exchange rates, and other technical matters had made it impossible for the South Manchurian Railway to make rate reductions automatically. A draft contract covering these matters was then being developed. Japan would be pleased to co-operate with American shipping lines in working out the details of the contract.[4]

Following this exchange, conversations were delayed several weeks while American shipping lines were consulted about the Japanese suggestion. The State Department was hopeful that the lines would negotiate with the Japanese, but the companies were not interested. The LaFollette Seaman's Bill had recently been enacted, and shippers, fearing that certain provisions would adversely affect their operations, were unwilling to enter new

[2] Lansing to Guthrie, *For. Rels.*, 1915, p. 617.

[3] Japanese Foreign Office to Post Wheeler, June 8, 1915, *For. Rels.*, 1915, p. 620. Wheeler to Bryan, June 9, 1915, SD 893.773/42.

[4] Y. Kubo to A. A. Williamson, May 18, 1915, *For. Rels.*, 1915, p. 621.

projects. Upon learning the companies' view, Japan notified the United States that she was suspending further consideration of the American protest.[5]

But the State Department refused to drop the matter. On January 25, 1916, Guthrie was instructed to lodge a protest which went over the same ground as the earlier one. Complaint was made against discriminatory treatment based on route of shipment, nationality of the carrying vessel, or signature of a contract between railway and shipping companies. Such treatment was alleged to be in violation of Japan's avowed intention to support the Open Door as well as her declarations on behalf of the principle of equal opportunity.[6]

The Japanese government was obviously irritated by this latest American protest. With respect to the first two points raised, Japan had made concessions many months earlier and had reaffirmed the concessions in the previous conversation with Guthrie. As for the complaint about the South Manchurian Railway's requiring a contract before extending a rates reduction, Japan had explained her position and had suggested a way out of the difficulty. According to Tokyo, the unresolved nature of the dispute was due more to the indifference of American companies than to Japanese intransigence. In short, it seemed to the Japanese that they had taken every reasonable step to satisfy American claims. The American persistence suggested that the United States was less interested in the alleged discriminatory treatment of American trade than in persuading the Japanese to declare their support of the principle of equal commercial and industrial opportunity. Thus, when Kikujiro Ishii, the Foreign Minister, replied to Guthrie, he gave renewed assurances of Japan's desire to take all practical steps to eliminate discriminatory treatment of American merchandise, but he was careful to pledge nothing beyond this. He failed to agree

[5] Guthrie to Lansing, Nov. 4, 1915, *For. Rels., 1915,* pp. 624-625.
[6] Lansing to Guthrie, *For. Rels.,* 1916 (Washington, 1925), pp. 446-447.

that the Open Door doctrine provided the United States with a basis for seeking redress on the points in question.[7]

Ishii's remarks were in line with previous Japanese responses to American protests. Throughout the freight rates controversy Japan indicated constant readiness to adjust practices which caused discriminatory treatment of American commerce. The adjustments, the Japanese averred, were made because of Japan's friendship for the United States. An analysis of the Japanese concessions suggests that Tokyo also acted out of consideration for the pledges which she made in response to the first Hay note. However, in responding to American protests Japan avoided reference to the Open Door. As was noted earlier, the Open Door had been defined in various ways by the United States. Japan was certainly aware of the shifting nature of the American definition and was prompted to act cautiously by its knowledge. A Japanese admission that a particular practice was a violation of the principle of equal opportunity would have been a step toward Japan's acceptance of a definition of the Open Door which did not admit the existence of spheres of influence. Since such a step would have carried Japanese policy backward, Tokyo was understandably anxious to avoid the use of American terminology in expressing its views on the freight rates controversy.

State Department records suggest that the Japanese suspicions of American aims were well grounded. During the early stages of the rates controversy, Lansing's concern was directed entirely toward the damage which might be done to American trade by discriminatory practices, but after April, 1915, the effort to protect American trade became a device for obtaining from Japan assent to a broad construction of the Open Door.[8] Indeed, when Guthrie's cable revealed that Ishii's statements did not satisfy the American purpose, another protest, almost identical with the last one, was prepared.[9] If this protest were de-

[7] Guthrie to Lansing, March 3, 1916, SD 893.773/46.
[8] Williams Memorandum, Jan. 7, 1916, SD 893.773/44.
[9] Frank Polk to Guthrie, *For. Rels.*, 1916, pp. 449-450.

livered, the fact was not recorded. At this point the papers relating to the controversy abruptly end. The sudden termination of correspondence should not be interpreted as evidence that the State Department either had abandoned its purpose or believed that its purpose was accomplished. More likely Lansing thought that little was to be gained by prolonging the matter. Japan had promised steps to safeguard American trade. As for the larger aim, Ishii's sidestepping of any reference to the Open Door suggested that Japan had perceived the American game and was unwilling to play it. If this were the case, reiteration of the American arguments would not elicit the desired view of the Open Door. Such tactics, however, would probably irritate Japan.[10]

Thus a minor episode in American-Japanese relations was terminated inconclusively. By extending the freight rates controversy beyond April, 1915, the State Department notified Japan that it was on guard against efforts to squeeze American trade from South Manchuria, but this was all that was accomplished. The concluding stages of the freight rates controversy have a place in the record of American diplomacy, however, because they were the first occasion during which Lansing sought to bridge the conflicting viewpoints noted earlier. As revealed in this episode, the Secretary's procedure had two sides. On one hand, the United States sought Japan's acceptance of a definition of the Open Door which embodied the principle of equal commercial and industrial opportunity and of the application of the Open Door thus defined to South Manchuria. The pursuit of such an aim was in line with the objectives of Wilson's policy. On the other hand, the American effort to bring Japan around to its point of view was conducted with utmost discretion. Nothing was said by the American Ambassador which indicated that the United States had determined finally its position toward South Manchuria. The imprecision of the United States on this latter point seems to have been calculated

[10] Guthrie to Lansing, March 3, 1916, SD 893.773/46.

to encourage Japan to make further inquiry about the possibility of striking a bargain with the American government. In a word, Lansing was laying the groundwork for alternative lines of action: steps could be undertaken by the United States to destroy the Japanese sphere, or Japan's claims to "special interest" could be admitted.

That this was indeed the Secretary's purpose was indicated by his reaction to the signature of treaties by Russia and Japan in July, 1916. Japan and Russia pledged publicly to assist each other in defending their interests in Manchuria. Both parties agreed to abstain from membership in any political arrangement which might be directed against the other. In the event of a menace to the "territorial rights or special interests" of one of the parties, there would be consultation to determine necessary measures. A secret treaty, which accompanied the public one, recognized that the "vital interests" of Japan and Russia demanded that China should not come under the influence of a "third power." Should such a development threaten, the parties would consider the use of military measures to obtain relief. When read together, these agreements constituted a defensive alliance which could be construed as being directed against the United States.

Attached to the alliance were several secret articles which were intended to speed Japan's penetration of South Manchuria. Russia agreed to open the Sungari River, part of which flowed through her sphere of influence, to Japanese vessels. This permitted shallow-draft gunboats to enter a complex river system and thereby cleared the way for effective control of the western areas of South Manchuria. Russia also agreed to sell to Japan a section of the Chinese Eastern Railway running between Changchun and Sungari stations. The sale was to give Japan access to a rich soya bean producing area.[11] In return for these concessions Japan was to supply arms to Russia.

[11] Japan may also have secured fishing rights off the Manchurian coast. Guthrie to Lansing, July 16, 1916, *For. Rels.*, 1916, p. 436. Final agreement on the articles relating to South Manchuria was probably not reached before

While the text of these secret agreements was not published until 1918, their substance was released immediately. The semiofficial *Manchuria Daily News,* which was the organ of the South Manchurian Railway, printed an outline of key articles. Presumably Japan was seeking to advise the powers of her intention to maintain and, indeed, expand her preferential position in South Manchuria. At least, the advice was so regarded in the United States. From Mukden, Manchuria, Consul General P. Stewart Heintzleman gave the State Department his analysis. The new treaties supplemented and broadened the Russo-Japanese agreements of 1907 and 1910, the instruments by which Russia and Japan agreed to divide Manchuria into spheres of influence. The terms of the earlier agreements made the recent understanding not at all surprising:

> It only discloses the weakened position of Russia in the Far East. That this is a diplomatic victory for Japan, who has not conceded anything on her part, is to be seen from the following inevitable result: the extension and strengthening of the political and strategic lines of the Japanese sphere of interests; on the other side the restricting of Russia's liberty of action in her sphere of interest and even in her territorial possessions in Eastern Asia. . . .[12]

Nor was the American press deceived by the agreement. Summaries of the Japanese press reports were carried in metropolitan papers. Editorials emphasized that Japan had strengthened her influence in South Manchuria, a development which was viewed darkly. The *New York Times* believed that American commercial development in Manchuria would be injured.[13] The New York *American* thought that the treaty meant Russia and Japan "had agreed to partition Asia between them and drive the United States out of the 'open door' and then shut and lock that door." The *Brooklyn Eagle* and New York *Evening Post* were similarly disapproving.[14]

---

the fall of the Czarist regime. They do not appear to have been put into effect. Dewitt C. Poole Memorandum, Oct. 19, 1921, SD 761.94/169.

[12] To Lansing, July 11, 1916, *For. Rels., 1916,* pp. 432-435.

[13] July 8, 1916.

[14] "More 'Peril' in the Far East," *Literary Digest,* LIII (July 22, 1916), 172.

The public discussion of the Russo-Japanese treaties prompted Lansing to make public the American response. On August 16 Lansing signed notes to Russia and Japan pointing out that the texts of the published convention failed to mention the preservation of China's administrative and territorial integrity. The United States desired the powers to reaffirm their adherence to these principles as they had done in the convention concluded by them in 1907.[15]

Viewed one way, the step was innocuous. The 1907 pledge had been vague and open to conflicting interpretations. It had not prevented Russia and Japan from establishing and consolidating their spheres of influence. Therefore, the reaffirmation would not invalidate any provisions of the treaties of 1916. Surely Lansing was aware of this. He had earlier noted that the Open Door was an almost meaningless term when applied to Manchuria. Certainly St. Petersburg and Tokyo must have regarded the desired statements as harmless. The pledges were promptly forthcoming from those cities.[16] In another sense, however, Lansing's action assumed importance. The request kept the American government on record as opposing the exercise of exclusive privileges in Manchuria. By thus keeping the record straight, the State Department maintained a position from which, if it so chose, it could move against the spheres in the future.[17]

The formula was similar to the one devised during the latter stages of the freight rates controversy. The American requests for reaffirmation of the Open Door were reservations of all American rights. The requests, however, implied no immediate threat to the status quo. The only new element was the spreading of the American action upon the public record. Clearly Lansing was still intent upon keeping open to the United States alternative lines of action. As we have seen, this intention was

[15] To David R. Francis and Guthrie, *For. Rels., 1916,* pp. 442-443.

[16] Guthrie to Lansing, Aug. 21, 1916; Francis to Lansing, Aug. 23, 1916, *For. Rels., 1916,* pp. 444-445.

[17] Williams Memorandum, Aug. 12, 1916, SD 761.94/127. William Phillips to Polk, July 12, 1916, Sterling Memorial Library, Yale University, The Papers of Frank L. Polk. Hereinafter cited as Polk Papers.

demonstrated twice with respect to Manchuria, but it was not confined to this region. Even as Lansing was dealing with the Russo-Japanese treaty settlement, the United States was under pressure to announce its position with respect to Japanese efforts to consolidate their claims to a sphere of influence in Eastern Inner Mongolia.

The occasion for the expression of American views on Japanese activities in Eastern Inner Mongolia was provided by a clash between Japanese and Chinese forces at Chengchiatun late in August, 1916. For several weeks prior to the clash, Japan had been sending troops into the area west of the South Manchuria Railway and south of the Sungari River. The troops were to reconnoiter and develop alliances with local Mongol tribes. By these means Japan intended to harass and effect the removal of Chinese authorities. When troops under the command of Chang Tso-lin, the energetic Chinese Governor of Manchuria, resisted the Japanese, a fight developed.[18]

Although the battle itself was of little consequence (there were ten Japanese casualties), Japan used the incident to press upon China a series of "requests and demands" which bore a marked resemblance to some of the postponed Twenty-one Demands. The "requests" were four in number: (1) Japanese military advisers were to be employed by the Chinese government in Manchuria and Inner Mongolia; (2) Japanese instructors were to be employed in Chinese military schools; (3) an indemnity was to be paid for the lives of Japanese soldiers who were killed at Chengchiatun; and (4) the Chinese government was to make a formal apology for the incident. To these were added an equal number of "demands": (1) a Japanese police service was to be established in parts of South Manchuria and Eastern Inner Mongolia where large numbers of Japanese resided; (2) Japanese advisers were to be attached to Chinese police forces throughout these regions; (3) all Chinese army

[18] Heintzleman to Lansing, Aug. 19, 27, 29, 1916, SD 793.94/525; 893.00/2344; 793.94/531.

officers who were involved in the incident were to be degraded in rank and dismissed from service; and (4) the Chinese government was to issue strict orders to its forces to avoid interference with Japanese military activities in South Manchuria. As had been the case in 1915, Japan enjoined China to the strictest secrecy. Peking, also adopting the tactics of the earlier occasion, conveyed unofficially the entire list of "requests and demands" to foreign powers and press representatives.[19]

From Mukden Heintzleman observed:

> The Japanese object is obviously to clear the region of Chinese troops by any means available, and as the region is known to be in a chronic state of disturbance, the Japanese will station troops there permanently. Out of this condition is to follow eventually the same state of affairs as exists in Outer Mongolia.[20]

Reinsch supported this interpretation and added the warning that China's acceptance of the "requests and demands" would set a precedent which Japan could use to subdue all of China. The United States, the Minister urged, should attempt to defeat Japan's purpose.[21]

The same line was taken by the American metropolitan press. Already aroused by the signature of the Russo-Japanese treaties, editors saw further infringement of American interests in the latest Japanese moves. The *New York Times,* regarded the proposed terms as violations of the Open Door.[22] The *Boston Herald* held the same view and suggested that a warning be given Japan. However, the *Herald* doubted that this would be the American policy: "The country has only a President's clerk at the State Department. Nothing will be done. No word will be spoken."[23]

[19] Reinsch to Lansing, Sept. 4, 1916, *For. Rels., 1916,* p. 241. *New York Times,* Aug. 20; Sept. 6, 1916.

[20] To Lansing, Sept. 6, 1916, SD 793.94/528. By 1916 Outer Mongolia was virtually a Russian protectorate, although Russia had formally recognized China's suzerainty over the area during the previous year.

[21] Reinsch to Lansing, Sept. 5, 1916, *For. Rels., 1916,* p. 243; SD; 793.94/519.

[22] Sept. 6, 1916.

[23] Sept. 6, 1916.

Amid these advices Lansing maintained an appearance of calmness. When questioned by reporters about the matter, he refused comment.[24] Privately, though, he showed some concern. On September 6 he inquired whether Britain planned any steps.[25] A note was also sent Japan asking the terms required of China. The United States, it was asserted, was entitled under the Root-Takahira notes to be informed in advance of any change in the status quo.[26]

Japan's reply was given in a conversation between Ishii and Guthrie. Ishii denied any obligation to inform the United States of her terms, but he volunteered to discuss the matter personally and informally so that no misunderstanding would arise. Japan did not intend to weaken Chinese authority. Rather, her purpose was to prevent the recurrence of an incident which had caused serious loss of life. Neither China's sovereignty, nor the principles of the Open Door would be impaired by the final settlement.[27] Lansing promptly released these assurances to the press. Once again he refused to comment officially, but the press reported that "semi-official" sources regarded Japan's disclaimer as "reassuring."[28] This ended the State Department's involvement in the Chengchiatun affair. Britain had informed the United States that she planned no steps.[29] The United States was unwilling to risk irritating the Japanese by being the only power to make a protest.

Late in January, 1917, China and Japan reached a tentative agreement. Chinese army officers were to be reprimanded; the Military Governor of Fengtien Province was to make a formal apology; Chinese soldiers and residents around Chengchiatun were to treat Japanese soldiers with courtesy; and a "consolation fee" of $500 was to be paid Japanese merchants who were

[24] *New York Times,* Sept. 6, 1916.
[25] Lansing to Page, SD 793.94/52a.
[26] Lansing to Guthrie, Sept. 6, 1916, *For. Rels., 1916,* p. 244.
[27] Guthrie to Lansing, Sept. 11, 1916, *For. Rels., 1916,* pp. 244-245.
[28] *New York Times,* Sept. 13, 1916.
[29] Irwin B. Laughlin to Lansing, Sept. 15, 1916, SD 793.94/526.

injured in the incident.[30] The more serious "requests and demands," i.e., those relating to Japanese police force, police advisers, and instructors in military academies, were dropped. By the middle of April final arrangements were completed, and the matter was closed.[31]

Japan's reasons for modifying her terms appear to have stemmed from internal political changes. The "requests and demands" were presented by the Okuma Ministry. On October 6, 1916, a new ministry was formed by General Count Seiki Terauchi. The new Premier proposed not to coerce China, but he was to seek enlargement of Japanese interests through political loans and corruption of Chinese officials. The final settlement doubtlessly reflected these intentions. China did not force a reduction of terms. Nor did the United States or Britain act to alter the outcome.

The relevance of this episode to the story of Lansing's diplomacy is not to be measured by America's lack of influence on the final settlement. Lansing did not try to change the outcome of the dispute. His aims were limited to two related things. He wished to maintain a position from which the United States could move against Japan's claims to "special interests." This was accomplished when Ishii gave assurances concerning the Open Door. He was also anxious to prevent publicity about Japan's "requests and demands" from creating a situation which might hinder an American-Japanese settlement or which would embarrass the United States at a time when she was moving toward war with Germany. The reasons for his concern require a word about the state of public opinion in the United States and Japan.

Following the outbreak of World War I, the American press, which had been decidedly anti-Japanese since the conclusion of

[30] John V. A. MacMurray, ed., *Treaties and Agreements with and Concerning China, 1894-1919* (New York, 1921), II, 1345. Hereinafter cited as MacMurray, *Treaties.*

[31] Edward C. Baker to Lansing, April 19, 1917, *For. Rels., 1917* (Washington, 1926), p. 258.

the Treaty of Portsmouth, assumed an increasingly hostile attitude toward Japan. Several minor incidents provided occasions for comment: Japanese merchants shipped arms to Mexican insurgents; fear of a Japanese attack on the Philippines was excited by Congressional debate over independence for those islands; and sporadic agitation against Japanese immigration had broken out. Newspapers devoted considerable space to Japan's invasion of Shantung and the Twenty-one Demands. These events nurtured suspicions which were expressed openly at the time of the Russo-Japanese treaty and Chengchiatun incident. The American press comment in turn sparked a reaction in the Japanese press. Early in 1916 Japanese newspapers began to transmit, frequently by cable at the cost of a dollar per word, to their home offices extracts from the American press. The extracts became the subject of angry rebuttals. The Japanese were particularly sensitive to American criticism of Japan's aims in Manchuria. Some of the more radical organs urged the government not to tolerate American interference.[32]

Lansing's efforts to end the sniping obtained mixed results. Following publication of Ishii's comments on the Open Door, the tone of American comment became less hostile, and the press dropped further coverage of Sino-Japanese negotiations.[33] Publication of the Japanese assurances, however, proved irritating to the Terauchi Ministry. Lansing's statement to the press carried the implication that the United States was imposing restraints on Japan. Japanese politicians could make use of the implication to embarrass the Ministry. Indeed, the danger of this was acute. Terauchi was preparing to reduce the terms to China. He could scarcely afford to appear to have made the move at America's behest. Thus, the final move in the Cheng-

[32] *New York Times,* Sept. 13, 1916; "How Japan Views our Mexican Troubles," *Literary Digest,* LIII (Sept. 16, 1916), 662. Guthrie to Lansing, July 17, 1916, *For. Rels., 1916,* pp. 438-439.

[33] Lansing to Guthrie, Oct. 23, 1916, SD 793.94/537. "Japan in the Doorway," *Literary Digest,* LIII (Oct. 28, 1916), 1095.

chiatun incident was a Japanese protest against Lansing's revelation of the content of Ishii's remarks to Guthrie.[34]

When the American response to the Chengchiatun incident and those relating to South Manchuria are viewed together, it becomes clear that between the summer of 1915 and the spring of 1917 Lansing was playing a waiting game. Would the United States concede its rights in South Manchuria and Eastern Inner Mongolia as part of a bargain with Japan, or would it be necessary to stick with Wilson's determination to oppose Japan's monopoly in those areas? Lansing did not know, and he felt that he should not press for a decision. Japan had not indicated that she would consider striking a bargain with the United States. Until she did, Lansing, always conscious of Wilson's determination to direct American policy, believed that little was to be gained by proposing a plan which was in opposition to the President's. Rather, his course was to be alert for an opportunity to bring his idea forward again, while maintaining a position from which the United States could move in either direction.

These tactics puzzled Japan. American protests concerning freight rates and requests for declarations on the Open Door were pinpricks. Did they foretell an American drive against the Japanese sphere of influence? On one hand, the failure of the United States to withdraw the assurances contained in the Note of March 13, 1915, suggested that the diplomacy described above was not intended for such a purpose. On the other, an opposite answer was indicated by the fact that America's Manchurian and Mongolian diplomacy was paralleled by a major effort to open China Proper to American investors. To understand Japan's concern over this latter development, it will be necessary to give an account of the American business program.

[34] Guthrie to Lansing, Sept. 25, 1916, SD 793.94/540 1/2.

7. Dollar Diplomacy

The American policy in China Proper contrasted sharply with the one followed in South Manchuria and Eastern Inner Mongolia. South of the Great Wall there was no indecisiveness in America's attitude toward spheres of influence. In 1915 the State Department began a program which was designed to destroy existing spheres and prevent the creation of new ones. This was attempted by inducing American capitalism to finance China's economic development and the reorganization of the Peking government. The program was sustained until early in 1917.

Lansing gave full support to the program. The Twenty-one Demands had convinced him that he must revise his thinking about American tactics. Prior to 1915 Japan seemed willing to limit her claims to "special interests" to Shantung, South Manchuria, and Eastern Inner Mongolia, but the text of the demands revealed much broader ambitions. Furthermore, as has been noted, Japanese pretensions had not encountered the resistance from European powers which Lansing had expected.[1] From these developments it appeared that the United States could not obtain economic opportunity in China by standing still. Lansing regarded his proposed bargain with Japan as one step toward the garnering of commercial opportunity. A second step

[1] The failure of the powers to co-operate against Japan was noted by several persons with the State Department. For example, see Reinsch to Bryan, Dec. 4, 1915, *Lansing Papers,* II, 429-430.

was to encourage Americans to increase substantially their stake in China.

The program through which the State Department sought to encourage investors grew out of suggestions made by Reinsch. From the beginning of his service in Peking, Reinsch had believed that large American investments in China would result in advantages to all parties. For Americans there would be profits. For the Chinese there would be stimulus for their national development. Young Chinese would be stimulated by their exposure to modern technology and American ideals, and the new American investment would crack the spheres of influence which had reduced China to a semi-colonial status. The result would be the gradual emergence of a modern state which would provide a better life for millions of its own people and a strong partner in the Pacific for the United States.[2] Upon returning to the United States late in May, 1915, for a vacation and consultation, Reinsch urged the State Department to encourage Americans to do business in China. Lansing listened sympathetically and referred the Minister to the Bureau of Foreign and Domestic Commerce. Within a few weeks the official program began to take shape.

State Department facilities were to be made available to American businessmen. Officials were to watch for business opportunities and supply interested firms with all pertinent information. The State Department's cables were to be opened to business communications, and diplomatic personnel were to aid

[2] The following is typical of Reinsch's sentiments: "The true ministers and ambassadors to China are the merchant adventurers of western nations, bearing their goods, their steel and tools. It was not for what the entrepreneurs could get out of China, nor yet what China could get out of us, that my policy as American Minister was directed to this meeting of two civilizations. It was because I saw millions, whose birthright in the higher arts and amenities of living is at least as rich as our own, perishing wretchedly for lack of an organizing and engineering skill that our western peoples can supply. . . . A little vision plus the scientific application of it would transform China."—Paul S. Reinsch, "American Merchant Adventurers in China," *Asia,* XXII (Feb., 1922), 106.

in the negotiation of contracts.[3] In performing these services, however, the State Department was not to become a party to any transactions. Nor was the government itself to give direct support to any activity in the sense that it would serve as a collecting agent or use force to coerce China into observing terms of a contract.

The development of this program coincided with a rising interest in foreign trade among American businessmen and financiers. Until this time the business community had been concerned chiefly with domestic enterprises, but circumstances growing out of the European war were producing a changed attitude. The withdrawal of European firms from the world market created enlarged opportunities. Trade in war material provided Americans with capital for investment abroad. By 1915 Americans anticipated capturing a large share of the world's business in Asia, Africa, and South America.[4]

An indication of this interest was the creation of a new kind of business organization. Late in 1915 Frank A. Vanderlip, President of the National City Bank of New York, and several other financial leaders formed the American International Corporation, which was to serve as fiscal agent for American firms doing business in foreign lands. It provided facilities for the analysis and investigation of business opportunities and also provided channels for the sale of foreign securities used to finance projects undertaken by American firms. In the latter respect the corporation was prepared to operate on a large scale. Provision was made for the marketing of up to $500,000,000 worth of securities at one time, and the corporation was prepared to expand this figure as circumstances required. The establishment

[3] An indication of the importance attached by the Department to this matter was to be seen in the recall of the Commercial Attaché from China to make a speaking tour. The Attaché was to inform businessmen of opportunities in China. See Frank F. Davis, "Broadening Our Chinese Trade," *Asia,* XVII (March, 1917), 41-43.

[4] *New York Times,* Nov. 23, 1915. The November 24 issue of the *Times* noted that the trade balance was running in America's favor at the rate of $2,000,000,000 annually.

of this organization had the effect of throwing open the overseas market to a large section of the business community. Most American firms did not have resources of their own to carry out the services just outlined.[5]

Significantly, Willard Straight was appointed Third Vice-President of the International Corporation. An earnest advocate of trade with China, Straight had been a key figure in the development of E. H. Harriman's scheme to build an American railway across Manchuria. Later he had been employed by the American Consortium Group to conduct negotiations in Peking. His association with the International Corporation was an augury that China was to be included in future ventures.

Sometime during the autumn of 1915 State Department officials were in touch with the International Corporation. The department desired to have the corporation consider two projects: the Huai River conservancy program and construction of fifteen hundred miles of railway. A few months later the department sought to interest bankers associated with the corporation in making direct loans to the Chinese government. Efforts to carry out these projects were to require attention for more than a year.

The Huai River water control program seemed an excellent place to begin the development of American investment. The existence of recent, detailed surveys meant that work could begin without much delay. The project itself was attractive. For the expenditure of $20,000,000, over a million acres of land which was capable of producing two crops annually could be placed in production. Revenue obtained from land sales and taxes would provide adequate security for a loan.[6] And finally, the work was desirable for political reasons. Americans would be establishing claims along the southwestern borders of Shan-

[5] *New York Times,* Nov. 23, 24, 25; Dec. 12, 1915.

[6] The surveys were carried out under the auspices of the Red Cross and New York banks which became interested in the project following a disastrous flood in 1911. For correspondence and engineering reports, see *For. Rels., 1914* (Washington, 1922), pp. 95-119.

tung, a region in which other projects could be expected to develop and where the United States would challenge British and Japanese claims of "special interests."

Happily for the State Department, little trouble was encountered in bringing together interested parties. The Peking government had long been anxious to have Americans undertake the work. Important links in China's railway and canal systems, which passed through the Huai River region, could be utilized by a power having selfish aims to spread her control over China. Peking was suspicious of European powers and Japan. The United States, on the other hand, had demonstrated to China's satisfaction, through her withdrawal from the Consortium, that she was desirous of preserving China's sovereignty. As evidence of her trust, Peking had given the American Red Cross an option on the conservancy project which could be taken up by American firms wishing to do the work. By late 1915 preliminary talks were being held by the Chinese government, the International Corporation, and Siems-Carey Railway and Canal Corporation.[7]

As the talks progressed, however, a series of obstacles appeared. The political turmoil arising out of Yuan Shih-k'ai's attempt to restore the monarchy made it unlikely that a loan of the size needed for the entire Huai project could be floated in the United States. The Americans, in consequence, urged that they be permitted to begin with a small section of the program.[8] China agreed and suggested the reconstruction of the part of the Grand Canal which ran through Shantung and Kiangsu Provinces.[9] Further delay was encountered in the spring of 1916

[7] Reinsch to Lansing, Oct. 25, 1915; Lansing to Reinsch, Nov. 6, 1915, SD 893.811/198. Paul S. Reinsch, *An American Diplomat in China* (Garden City, 1922), pp. 80-82. Hereinafter cited as Reinsch, *American Diplomat.*

[8] Lansing (for the Int. Corp.) to Reinsch, Dec. 17, 28, 1915, SD 893.811/201.

[9] Reinsch to Lansing, Jan. 4, 1916; Feb. 4, 1916, *For. Rels., 1916,* pp. 103-104. The section of canal connecting the Hwang and Yangtze rivers formed part of the outlet of the Huai River. For information on the economic significance of the work, see Reinsch to Lansing, Jan. 4, 1916, *For. Rels.,*

when Kiangsu officials, jealously guarding their own local authority, refused to approve the contract terms. Since American bankers doubted the ability of the Peking government to execute a contract in the face of local opposition, they insisted that further talks be postponed until the Chinese resolved the question of conflicting jurisdiction.[10] This problem was not resolved when still another difficulty appeared in the form of a Japanese protest. Under terms of the Sino-German Agreement of 1898, which concerned the lease of Kiaochow, China pledged to German capitalists and merchants an option on all construction done in Shantung Province which required the use of foreign labor, material, or capital. In the Treaties and Notes of May, 1915, China pledged to recognize any arrangement that might be made by Germany and Japan regarding the transfer of the former power's rights, interests, and concessions in China to the latter power. Resting her claim on these instruments, Japan protested to the Chinese government late in September, 1916, against the canal contracts. Japan claimed that China was obligated to offer the project to Japanese financiers and contractors.[11]

China quickly contested the Japanese claim. German rights and privileges, it was asserted, would not accrue to Japan until formal provision was made for their transfer. Thus far, this step had not been taken. Until it was, China regarded her agreement with Germany to be in force. As evidence of this fact, China had offered the canal project to Germany before entering negotiations with Americans.[12] Furthermore, even if Japan did possess German rights and privileges, she would have no legal right to interfere in the canal project. While the 1898 agreement had conferred upon Germany broad privileges in the development of Shantung, those privileges had been exercised only for

1916, p. 103; and "Improvement of the Grand Canal," *Far Eastern Review,* XIII (Aug. 1916), 100-101.

[10] Lansing to Reinsch, June 15, 1916, *For. Rels., 1916,* p. 119.

[11] Reinsch to Lansing, Sept. 25, 1916, *For. Rels., 1916,* p. 123.

[12] Reinsch to Lansing, May 24, 1916, SD 893.811/217.

construction of railways and exploitation of mineral resources. Japan was thus estopped by practice from claiming special preference in Shantung, except with respect to those two specific types of enterprises. All other kinds of projects were open to all nations on an equal basis.[13] Several weeks after this note went forward, on November 6, 1916, Lansing instructed Reinsch to give full support to the Chinese position.[14]

China's quick response and America's unqualified support of the Chinese position suggests that the two governments had made plans in advance of the Japanese protest. Claims of "special privilege" were to be met with the argument that failure to exercise general rights and privileges brought about their cancellation. This was a novel view, one which the powers had never admitted in practice. However, it is doubtful that Lansing relied on precedent to win the case. In 1914 the Secretary had predicted that European powers would admit Americans to their spheres to block Japanese expansion. Now, two years later, he gave support to a view of spheres of influence which, if accepted, would permit such a development. We shall note shortly that this view was presented to Britain, France, and Russia as well as to Japan. Clearly, Lansing hoped to obtain European support. In this way Japan would be under pressure to accept a limited definition of "special privilege."[15]

Lansing's instructions were significant in two additional respects. In the first place, the view of spheres of influence expressed here differed from the one Lansing held with respect to South Manchuria and Eastern Inner Mongolia. Indeed, it will later appear that he blocked an effort by Reinsch to challenge Japan's claim to exclusive investment privileges in South Manchuria. Here is evidence that Lansing distinguished between

[13] Reinsch to Lansing, Sept. 25, 1916, *For. Rels., 1916,* p. 123.

[14] *For. Rels., 1916,* p. 127.

[15] American officials were fully aware that the view advanced of the spheres of influence did not accord with practice. Lansing's note can be interpreted only as a deliberate attack on the Japanese sphere. See Williams to State Department Solicitors, April 4, 1917, attached to Reinsch to Lansing, April 3, 1917, SD 893.77/1594.

China Proper and South Manchuria and Eastern Inner Mongolia in directing American diplomacy. Secondly, Lansing's instructions mark a shift in his thinking about Japan's claims in Shantung. The March 13 Note indicated a willingness to recognize Japan's "special interests" in that province. Such indications were now withdrawn. Completion of the canal contracts would establish important American commercial interests in Shantung. Not only did the project promise to be profitable in itself, it was also an opening through which the United States might gain entry into larger, even more profitable, projects. These factors, which had not figured in Lansing's earlier consideration of the Shantung question, prompted the reversal in the Secretary's position. Lansing's instructions to Reinsch mark the beginning of an effort sustained through the Paris Peace Conference to rout the Japanese efforts to take over the German sphere of influence. It should be noted that from Lansing's viewpoint the effort grew out of a plan to expand America's commercial interests in China, rather than an altruistic desire to uphold China's integrity.

Lansing's diplomatic offensive was scarcely begun when complications in the form of a shift in Japanese strategy appeared. Japan did not continue to oppose the entry of American capital into their sphere of influence. Rather, Japanese representatives informed the International Corporation that the Bank of Japan would like to share in financing the canal project.[16] This move, which came in early January, 1917, was a sharp departure from the previous Japanese position. Its origins and impact on the American program deserve an explanation.

The formation of the Terauchi Ministry in October, 1916, brought into office men who were critical of the Okuma foreign policy. Okuma's efforts to establish close ties between China and Japan were approved, but it was felt that the tactics employed to obtain this end had resulted in little accomplishment and much harm. The invasion of Shantung and Twenty-one De-

[16] Reinsch to Lansing, Jan. 2, 1917, *For. Rels., 1917,* p. 207.

mands had aroused great resentment in China. Japanese trade with China had, in consequence, suffered injury. Moreover, these actions had resulted in strained relations with the United States. This was unfortunate. Trade with the United States was vital to Japan's welfare. The American market absorbed increasing quantities of Japanese manufactured cotton goods. Japan was dependent upon the United States for raw cotton, metals, and machinery. Key Japanese businessmen believed that the economic boom, which had developed following the outbreak of war, would collapse if Japan were deprived of this American commerce. The problem, then, for the Terauchi Ministry, was to discover a way to pursue Okuma's objectives without encountering his difficulties.

The plan that was adopted appears to have had its origins in the suggestions made by certain men who were prominent in financial and official circles. Shortly after the outbreak of war, Ei-uchi Shibusawa, Yosahiro Sakatani, Kentaro Kaneko, and Dr. Sho Den led the cry for a change in Japan's China policy. They urged that the "coercion" of China be ended; that Japanese influence be extended through trade, investment, and loans. In following the latter course, it would be advantageous to co-operate with the United States. Japan, in spite of her boom, could not match American resources in investment capital or heavy industry. Open competition between the countries would result in Americans gaining a preponderant share of the China market. The most feasible means of eliminating this danger would be to encourage the combination of Japanese and American resources. Co-operation would provide the means for controlling and directing American energies.[17] The fall of the Okuma Ministry was due partly to this campaign. The new Ministry included exponents of a conciliatory policy toward China and the United States.[18]

[17] Guthrie to Lansing, Aug. 1; Sept. 25, 1916, SD 793.94/538 1/2, 540 1/2.

[18] Guthrie to Lansing, Nov. 27, 1916, SD 793.94/544. The observations of the American Ambassador have been supported by recent research. See

The proposal to combine American and Japanese resources was made at a time when American bankers had become deeply concerned by the risks involved in going forward with the canal project. The war lords in Peking had failed to establish a regime whose authority was respected. Civil strife threatened to impede, if not destroy, construction work. Moreover, the Japanese had made clear their opposition to Americans doing the work alone. Against these dangers the bankers had little defense. The American government, which was bound by Wilson's determination to avoid any infringement of China's integrity, was unlikely to go beyond diplomatic means in supporting the project, and diplomacy, the bankers thought, did not offer sufficient protection. The Japanese offer, on the other hand, did provide a measure of security. The Japanese would not interfere in a project in which they had a part. Japan was also in a position to insist on strict observance by the Chinese of the terms of the loan contract.[19] These considerations prompted the International Corporation to accept the proffered cooperation with Japan.[20]

The Chinese and American governments, which were not informed in advance of the International Corporation's decision, were irritated by the entry of Japan into the canal project. The step defeated one of the major purposes of the program, the prevention of Japanese expansion into China Proper. Instead of erecting a barrier to the westward extension of Japanese interests from Shantung, the canal project would serve as a vehicle for Japanese penetration of Kiangsu Province. Reinsch, who relayed Peking's expressions of concern to Washington, commented angrily, "It would have been impossible to find a more unsuitable enterprise for co-operation."[21] Lansing was similarly

Frank C. Langdon, "Japan's Failure to Establish Friendly Relations with China in 1917-1918," *Pacific Historical Review,* XXVI (Aug. 1957), 245-258.

[19] This view was frequently expressed by Americans doing business in China. See Williams H. Williams, "An American-Asiatic Business Program," *Asia,* XVII (April, 1917), 132-134.

[20] American International Corporation to its representatives in Peking, Feb. 5, 1917, *For. Rels., 1917,* p. 210

[21] To Lansing, Jan. 2, 1917, *For. Rels., 1917,* p. 207.

chagrined. In an interview with Willard Straight he urged the International Corporation to reverse its decision. The department, Lansing observed, was not opposed to joint enterprises in China, but it hoped that American and Japanese financiers would work together on some other project.[22] The pleading did no good. The American bankers were not persuaded to renounce their agreement with the Japanese.

While Lansing was disappointed, he did not attempt to block the co-operative enterprise. If the State Department attempted to force the International Corporation to go forward without the Japanese, the firm might drop the project or experience difficulties in floating a loan because of Japanese opposition. In either event this would likely result in the Japanese taking over the entire project. Such a prospect was more forbidding than a co-operative venture. The only feasible course was to encourage the International Corporation to complete arrangements with Japanese bankers.[23]

Early in 1917 the International Corporation and Bank of Japan opened negotiations with the Chinese government. Revisions were made in the original contracts. The section of the Grand Canal running through Chihli Province was substituted for the one in Kiangsu. The project was to be financed by a $6,000,000 gold loan floated jointly by Americans and Japanese. Japanese supervisory personnel were to work with the Siems-Carey Construction Company.[24] These changes were completed by November, 1917, and the contract was approved by the Chinese government. Privately, Chinese officials expressed displeasure with the contract terms, but they dared not to reject them lest Japan take over the entire project.[25]

[22] Lansing to Reinsch, Jan. 8, 1917, *For. Rels., 1917,* pp. 207-208.

[23] Lansing to Reinsch, January 13, 1917; April 10, 1917, *For. Rels., 1917,* pp. 208, 215.

[24] MacMurray, *Treaties,* II, 1287-1291.

[25] Reinsch to Lansing, Aug. 30, 1917, *For. Rels., 1917,* p. 220. Long Memorandum, Dec. 3, 1917, "Memoranda, China, January 31, 1917-May 31, 1918," The Papers of Breckenridge Long, Library of Congress. Hereinafter cited as the Long Papers.

The conclusion of the contract brought a suspension of further consideration of the canal project. Even before negotiations were completed, the International Corporation lost interest. The American declaration of war in 1917 served to accelerate an already booming war trade. The Corporation's financial resources could be invested with more profit and less risk in places other than China. Indeed, only pressure from Lansing caused Corporation officials to complete contract negotiations. Lansing was aware of the Corporation's attitude, but it was desirable to have the contract signed. American firms would be assured of an option on the canal work when circumstances were propitious.[26] Thus a key phase of the State Department's investment program was terminated on an indecisive note. Early hopes for the establishment of a major American enterprise in China were disappointed, but an opening remained through which American capital might enter. In 1917 Lansing was still hopeful that Americans would make use of this opening.

The inauguration of the American effort to crack the spheres of influence placed one of Lansing's key assumptions on trial. The Secretary had predicted that European powers would co-operate with the United States in helping to establish American capital interests. These powers, fearing the extension of Japanese monopoly, would open their spheres of influence to investors. An opportunity to test the accuracy of this prediction came in 1916 and 1917. While negotiations over the Grand Canal contract were in progress, the International Corporation and Siems-Carey Company co-operated with the Peking regime in an effort to establish a plan for railway construction in China. Out of these discussions came agreements to build three lines which crossed territory claimed as spheres of influence by Russia, Britain, and France.

Preliminary contracts for construction of the lines were signed on May 17, 1916. The agreement called for the laying

[26] Lansing to the American International Corporation, Sept. 14, 1917, *For. Rels., 1917*, p. 222.

of 1,500 miles of track in widely separated parts of China. One line was to run from Kwei-Sui in north Shanshi Province along the Hwang River to Lan-chow in Kansu Province; a second line was to connect the important trade marts of Kai-feng in Honan Province and Suchow in Anhwei Province; and the third was to traverse the territory between Hanchow and Wenchow in Chekiang Province. The International Corporation was to finance the work with loans secured upon revenues obtained from the railways after they were in operation.[27]

The railway scheme encountered immediate opposition. Early in August Russia lodged a protest in Peking against the construction of the Shanshi-Kansu line on the ground that she was entitled to preference in railway construction in northern China. The protest was supported by reference to notes exchanged by China and Russia in 1899 which provided that only Russian firms and capital were to be employed in building railways in the vicinity of Peking.[28]

Upon learning of the protest, Lansing indicated that the American government would give full diplomatic support to the Sino-American contract.[29] The argument advanced rested on two points. First, the Sino-Russian notes did not provide a valid claim against the American contract. China had assented to Russia's building railroads only in a north or northeasterly direction from Peking. The proposed road was to run in a southwesterly direction.[30] Second, Russia's claim was in conflict with her repeated declarations of support for the Open Door and integrity of China. In view of the declarations, the United States was

[27] Text of the contract is printed in *For. Rels., 1916,* pp. 183-188. After reviewing the contract, the International Corporation ratified it in June. Lansing to Reinsch, June 15, 1916, *For. Rels., 1916,* p. 120. Later some adjustments were made in track location and mileage. Reinsch to Lansing, Oct. 27; Nov. 15; Dec. 19, 1916; Jan. 31; Feb. 1, 1917, SD 893.77/1569,1573, 1577, 1578, 1579.

[28] Reinsch to Lansing, Aug. 10, 1916, *For. Rels., 1916,* pp. 188-189.

[29] Lansing to Reinsch, Aug. 12, 1916, *For. Rels., 1916,* p. 189.

[30] Reinsch to Lansing, Oct. 31, 1916, *For. Rels., 1916,* p. 200.

bound to recognize Russian rights only insofar as those rights were based upon specific grants and concessions from China.[31]

The Russian protest was followed by notes from France and Britain. These latter countries protested against construction of the railway lines in Chekiang and Honan Provinces. Both claimed exclusive privilege based on concessions made secretly by local Chinese officials.[32] In replying to these protests the United States used the familiar line. Concessions that were not ratified by the Peking government could not defeat a public contract. Moreover, the United States did not recognize claims to special preference of a general character because they conflicted with repeated declarations of support for the Open Door.[33]

The exchanges with Russia and France were fruitless. Neither country made concessions to the American view. The reply from Britain, however, was promising. On September 8, 1917, the British Ambassador handed Lansing a memorandum which concluded with the following significant remarks:

> The Department of State may possibly argue that by the recognition of all existing agreements and declarations with regard to railway concessions in China, American enterprise would be debarred from the construction of a number of remunerative lines, which the agreements and declarations cover, but which the nationals of the powers concerned are unable or unwilling to construct. In the case of the British concessions which might be included in this category, the railways involved are trunk lines of great importance, the failure of the British concessionaires to construct them being solely due to the financial burden which Great Britain has been called on to bear in connection with the European war. *It is clear that the lines in question should be constructed at the earliest possible moment in the interests of China and of foreign trade, and, in the event of funds still being available in the United States for such a purpose, His Majesty's Government would be the first to*

[31] Lansing to Reinsch, Nov. 2, 1916, *For. Rels., 1916,* p. 205.

[32] Reinsch to Lansing, April 3; July 14, 1917, *For. Rels., 1917,* pp. 183-184, 190.

[33] Reinsch to Lansing, April 13, 1917; Lansing to French Ambassador, May 1; Aug. 24, 1917; Lansing to British Ambassador, Aug. 24; Sept. 20, 1917, *For. Rels., 1917,* pp. 184, 188, 191, 193-194, 197-198.

welcome the co-operation of British and American interests in their construction.[34]

The implication was clear. The British were disposed to admit American capital to their sphere on a basis of co-operation with British firms.[35] America's response was prompt. The United States, Lansing assured the Ambassador, would be glad to encourage co-operative ventures between American and British firms.[36]

As was the case with the canal project, however, these diplomatic exchanges marked a suspension of work. The American International Corporation had lost interest in doing business in China. Moreover, the prospect of British and American co-operation in the construction of railways raised questions about the validity of the International Corporation's contracts. These contracts touched options held by certain British, American and other foreign bankers for the construction of the "Hukuang railways," a project which had been started several years earlier.[37] The resulting legal difficulties needed to be unraveled before construction could start. Since the United States was by then a participant in the war against Germany, harried officials had not the time or energy to pursue the work. The suspension did not, however, signify a lack of interest in the State Department in the railway project. Lansing recognized that the British had acted in the way he had predicted. He intended to press his advantage at the earliest opportunity. The ways he chose to do this will be taken up at a later point in our story.

Direct loans to the Peking government formed a third phase of the American investment program in China. On November 16, 1916, the Chicago Continental and Commercial Trust and Savings Bank, having encouragement from the State Depart-

[34] *For. Rels., 1917,* pp. 195-196. Italics are mine.

[35] Williams to Lansing, May 14, 1918, Long Papers, "Memoranda, China, 1917-1918."

[36] Lansing to the British Ambassador, Sept. 20, 1917, *For. Rels., 1917,* pp. 197-198.

[37] The proposed railway was to run through Hupei and Hunan Provinces. For the text of the agreement see MacMurray, *Treaties,* I, 874-875.

ment, agreed to advance Chinese officials $5,000,000 and to consider a further loan of $25,000,000. From the American standpoint the move was designed to help stabilize the regime with which the International Corporation was negotiating about canal and railway projects. From the Japanese standpoint the loan raised further questions about American intentions in China.

Loans to the Peking government were apparently not a part of the plans drawn by the State Department in the summer of 1915. Wilson had made clear his dislike of them. They provided outside interests with an opportunity to exercise control over the Chinese. As a practical matter, however, the State Department found it necessary to consider such loans in the summer of 1916. Civil disorder in China had almost stopped the flow of revenue to Peking. Japan had offered Peking funds to meet her needs and had suggested that China designate Japan as her fiscal agent.[38] Thus, Tokyo was threatening to dominate China by making her financially dependent on Japan. The prospect did not favor the development of American interests in China. With Peking under Japanese influence, American firms would be unlikely to obtain contracts. To keep China open to American investment, the United States would have to find a means for countering Japan's tactics.

Lansing favored doing this by reviving the old American Consortium Group and asking it to make a loan to China through the Six Power Consortium. Action along this line had decided advantages. For one thing, estimates placed Peking's needs at $45,000,000.[39] Consortium channels provided the only means of making such a large loan quickly. A second advantage stemmed from the reactivation of the Consortium itself. Member nations had agreed to give Consortium bankers a monopoly over administrative loans to China. Since Japan was a member,

[38] Reinsch to Lansing, June 15, 1916, SD 893.51/1652.

[39] One-third of the sum was for restoration of bank credit; the remainder was to be used for governmental reorganization. Reinsch to Lansing, May 26, 1916, SD 893.51/1644.

the operation of the Consortium would check Japanese efforts to increase their influence in Peking through independent loans. Furthermore, the scheme had a good chance of being put into effect. The National City Bank of New York, a member of the old Group, was urging its foreign colleagues to undertake business with China once again. Britain, France, and Russia would probably favor an American effort to revive the Consortium. These countries, which appeared increasingly interested in controlling Japanese expansion, would exert pressure on Japan to co-operate with the Consortium. All of these considerations were outlined in a letter written by Lansing and addressed to Wilson on June 15, 1916.[40] Wilson responded by approving Lansing's recommendation with only one qualification: the American government was not to act as guarantor of the loan.[41] By the end of June department officials were meeting with Consortium bankers.

These efforts were to end in frustration. At first delays arose from squabbles among the American bankers over the membership of the Group.[42] By the time these were resolved the waning interest of the National City Bank (also a leader in the American International Corporation) in doing business in China caused negotiations to collapse.[43] This result did not shake Lansing's belief in the usefulness of the Consortium as an instrument of American policy. Later he was to return to the idea of using that organization to control Japan. The collapse of talks, however, forced the Secretary to devise other means for furnishing financial aid to China.

Efforts were made to interest several banks in negotiating

[40] SD 893.51/1652. See also Williams Memorandum, June 26, 1916, SD 893.51/1696; Polk Memorandum, n. d. [June, 1916], Polk Papers.

[41] Wilson to Lansing, June 21, 1916, SD 893.51/3009.

[42] The quarrel arose out of claims advanced by Lee, Higginson and Company of Boston. For details of the dispute and terms of settlement, see the memoranda and correspondence under the following file numbers: SD 893.51/1696, 1652, 1665. Also see William Phillips to Polk, July 12, 13, 1916, Polk Papers and entries for June and July, 1916, in "Diary," Polk Papers.

[43] Polk to Reinsch, Aug. 5, 1916, SD 893.51/1672.

separate loans to Peking. Only the Chicago bank responded to the State Department's entreaties. Shortly after the contract was signed with Peking, the Chicago bank transferred the proceeds of the $5,000,000 to China and opened talks looking toward the flotation of the larger loan.[44] For a while Lansing was hopeful that these talks would be successful, but, again, Japanese opposition was encountered.

Late in November France, which was evidently acting under Japanese pressure, protested against the Chicago loan contract. The contract was claimed to be invalid because it was secured on proceeds of the tobacco and wine tax. A French bank already held a lien on these proceeds.[45] Simultaneously, Japan persuaded Britain, France, and Russia to join her in protesting that the loan infringed China's obligations under the Reorganization Loan contract of 1913. China was bound by this agreement to make all administrative and reorganizational loans through the Consortium.[46] On January 15, 1917, Japan warned Peking against completing the Chicago loan. If China would abandon negotiations, Tokyo promised a Japanese loan of Yen 10,000,000 and additional funds whenever they were needed.[47] Meanwhile the Japanese Ambassador in Washington informed news reporters that Japan would not countenance a loan which would give Americans control over certain Chinese enterprises.[48] This latter declaration was interpreted in the State Department as a direct warning to the Chicago bank.[49]

Lansing acted promptly to offset these moves. Reinsch was instructed to tell the interested ministers that "any strained construction of existing agreements between the Chinese Government and bankers, or any attempt to exclude our Bankers from a fair participation in Chinese affairs, would meet with decided

[44] Statement by Jay Abbott of the Chicago bank. MacMurray, *Treaties,* II, 1343.

[45] Reinsch to Lansing, Nov. 29, 1916, *For. Rels., 1916,* pp. 143-145.

[46] *Ibid.*

[47] Reinsch to Lansing, Jan. 15, 1917, *For. Rels., 1917,* p. 116.

[48] *Washington Post,* Jan. 17, 1917.

[49] Lansing to Wilson, Jan. 17, 1917, SD 893.51/1746a.

resistance from this Government."[50] This display of firmness obtained a measure of success. The Western powers, which were perhaps reluctant to make the protest in the first place, showed no inclination to press the matter.[51]

But the Secretary's action failed to assure the Chicago bankers. The existing disorder in China would make it easy for Japan to foment a revolution against Peking if her wishes were ignored. This greatly increased the risks to investors, which the American government could do little to alleviate. In accordance with established policy the United States would employ only diplomatic means to protect investors. These facts were well understood by the Chicago bankers. Encouraged by the State Department, they continued negotiations throughout much of 1917, but they were clearly no longer greatly interested in the project. The affair ended with the bank's refusing to float the loan.[52]

By January, 1917, Lansing recognized that his early expectations of the successful establishment of American enterprise in China were not to be realized.[53] He had hoped that the department's investment program would bring quick results. Negotiations over canal, railway, and loan contracts were continuing, but no new American business appeared ready to go into China. The firms were completing contracts only because the State Department urged them to do so. The enthusiasm of the International Corporation and other firms for business with China had begun to disappear in the autumn of 1916. Lacking the initiative of businessmen, there was nothing the State Department could do to effect the immediate establishment of large scale investments.

Lansing had expected difficulties in the form of opposition from the powers claiming spheres of influence, and had formulated plans to cope with them. These, however, were not the

[50] Lansing to Reinsch, Dec. 5, 1916, *For. Rels., 1916,* p. 146.
[51] Reinsch to Lansing, Dec. 18, 1916, *For. Rels., 1916,* pp. 148-149.
[52] *For. Rels., 1917,* pp. 120-130, contains correspondence on this question.
[53] Lansing to Wilson, Jan. 17, 1917, SD 893.51/1746a.

only obstacles to appear. Hostilities in Europe created vast new investment opportunities for American capitalists. At the same time, Yuan Shih-k'ai's regime, which had given China the appearance of stability in 1915, had crumbled. The regimes which followed were unable to maintain order. The impact of these events was graphically portrayed in a communication from Lee, Higginson and Company, an investment firm, to the State Department:

> We appreciate fully that the failure to secure a loan for China in the United States at this time may have a far reaching effect on the future trade relations between the two countries, but we are not in any way to blame for the causes which have made it impossible for us . . . to carry on successfully a campaign of education of the American investing public.
>
> [For many months] . . . there has been a steady stream of press cables from China reporting revolutions, rebellions and friction between China and Japan. At the same time, our security markets have been under pressure to take securities from every part of the world by nations whose credit is either unquestioned or who could give collateral security of a tangible nature.
>
> Our advice, therefore, to the Chinese Minister has been consistently that unless his Government could give security that the American investing public would be willing to accept, they must wait until the public could be educated to take their bonds and that such a campaign of education could not begin until things had quieted down in China.[54]

From this it appears that, in part, Lansing's hopes had foundered on difficulties which could be neither entirely anticipated, nor controlled by the American government.

While the State Department's investment program did not fulfil all expectations, it would be wrong to regard it as a total failure. There was significant accomplishment. Japan had retreated from her initial opposition to the entry of American capital into Shantung and had offered to share in the enterprise. The British had hinted broadly that they would not object to American investment in their sphere of influence. Discussions of

[54] To Alvin A. Adee, Sept. 6, 1916, SD 893.51/1687.

reviving the China Consortium had provided evidence of a willingness on the part of European powers to co-operate with the United States to control Japanese expansion in China. In a word, opportunities were opened for future investment. The State Department's campaign had cleared away some, though by no means all, of the obstacles to the enlargement of American interests. Lansing recognized what had been done. In formulating American policy during the remainder of his term in office, he was to seek to capitalize on the accomplishments just described.

In another respect, however, Lansing must have been less satisfied with the results of the American business program. The United States had challenged claims to "special interests" in China Proper, including those advanced by Japan in Shantung. Tokyo was certain to link these moves with the already described American diplomacy in South Manchuria and Eastern Inner Mongolia. When viewed together, these two aspects of American policy would probably be regarded as an effort to eliminate Japanese influence in China. The resulting strains in American-Japanese relations might destroy the chance for making the bargain Lansing had in mind. As it developed, whatever worries Lansing may have had in this connection did not disappear with the collapse of the business program. During the early months of 1917, Reinsch, acting without the sanction of Lansing and Wilson, contributed still another chapter to the story of developing American-Japanese tension.

8. China's Devoted Friend

Reinsch was outraged by the blows dealt the American investments program. His desire to assist in developing China and bringing her into close association with the United States did not disappear in the face of difficulties. Indeed, if continued Chinese civil disorder, Japanese opposition to American programs, and evidence of timidity among American bankers may be said to have had any effect on the Minister, they aroused his determination. To Reinsch, failure did not cast doubt on the desirability or practicality of his aims. It meant only that new measures must be devised. Thus, early in 1917 he set himself to the task. The Japanese protest against American construction in Shantung was met with a threat to force American capital into South Manchuria. Japan's growing influence in Peking was countered with the offer to Chinese officials of a Sino-American alliance. Neither of these moves was sanctioned by the State Department, nor did they obtain the result Reinsch anticipated. In both cases Lansing disavowed the Minister's action. This did not mean, however, that these events had little importance in American-Japanese relations. Quite the contrary. Within the Wilson administration the question of how to deal with an expanding Japan was raised anew; and Lansing was thus provided with a fresh opportunity to urge the adoption of his bargain. Japan, now deeply concerned by the developing

American challenge, was persuaded by Reinsch's maneuvers that it was time to settle her differences with the United States.

Reinsch's attack on Japan's spheres of influence was launched on January 3, 1917. The Minister had recently learned of the proposal to have Americans and Japanese co-operate on the Grand Canal project. Seeking to counter this idea, he suggested the substitution of a jointly constructed railway in South Manchuria. Americans already held a concession for a railway between Chinchow and Aigun. Furthermore, Peking would be more inclined to approve a Manchurian project than one in Shantung.[1] Japan's response to this argument was to inform Reinsch that the validity of the Chinchow-Aigun concession was not admitted and to refuse to discuss the matter with him.[2]

This reply was indicative only of Japan's desire to circumvent Reinsch, not a lack of concern over American intentions. Japan was in fact greatly concerned. The reference to the Chinchow-Aigun project revived unpleasant memories of the Taft administration's effort to smoke Japan out of South Manchuria. Only recently Japan had been informed of the American intention to withdraw her proffered recognition of Japan's "special interests" in Shantung. Did Reinsch's proposal signify further modification of the March 13, 1915, Note? To learn the answer, the Japanese Ambassador called on Lansing on January 25. The Secretary emphatically denied having any advance knowledge of Reinsch's proposal and said further:

> . . . the Ambassador must surely be aware that the American Government recognized that Japan had special interests in Manchuria. Although no declaration to that effect had been made by the United States yet this Government had repeatedly shown a practical recognition of the fact and did not desire to do anything there to interfere with Japan's interests.

Later in the conversation Lansing called attention to the difference in America's attitude toward Manchuria, where Japan's

[1] Reinsch to Lansing (enclosing a copy of Reinsch's note), *For. Rels., 1917*, pp. 168-169.

[2] Japanese Minister to Reinsch, January 20, 1917, *For. Rels., 1917*, p. 172.

"special interests were conceded, and Shantung, where no such special interest was recognized."[3] The passage of two years had not altered Lansing's thinking. A bargain on China remained an essential part of a settlement between the United States and Japan.

Wilson's reaction to Lansing's remarks presents a puzzle for historians. After reading Lansing's memorandum of the talk, he wrote the Secretary, "I think the position you took the right one throughout the conversation."[4] Such unqualified approval is surprising. As has been noted, after April, 1915, Wilson became increasingly determined to prevent the strengthening of a Japanese regime of "special privilege" in South Manchuria. Except for the statement just quoted, there is no evidence to suggest an abatement of this determination. Indeed, one of the considerations which appears to have prompted Wilson to approve later the sending of American troops to Siberia was his desire to uphold the integrity of Manchuria. Thus the President's reasons for approving Lansing's position remain obscure. This, however, did not alter the effect of the approval. Lansing had obtained a sanction to pursue his plans.

But Wilson's comment did not close the matter. Reinsch was indignant at the Secretary's behavior. He sent strongly worded cables to the department arguing that Lansing's views were incorrect. The United States, Reinsch insisted, had never given formal recognition to Japan's claim to preferential rights in South Manchuria and Eastern Inner Mongolia. Japan's rights and privileges were based upon certain specific grants and concessions made by China. Under its treaties with China the

[3] Lansing Memorandum, *For. Rels., 1917,* p. 117. Lansing later maintained in a cable to Reinsch that these remarks were not intended to imply a willingness to recognize Japan's claim to general preference. He meant only to distinguish between South Manchuria, where the United States recognized specific Japanese concessions, and Shantung, where no such Japanese claims were recognized. Lansing to Reinsch, April 16, 1917, *For. Rels., 1917,* p. 187. Lansing did not convey this interpretation of his remarks to the Japanese, who had obtained quite another meaning from them.

[4] Wilson to Lansing, Jan. 31, 1917, SD 893.51/1743.

United States was entitled to share in these rights and privileges.[5] These arguments terminated in an apparent victory for the Minister. The State Department's Counselor, Frank L. Polk, cabled Reinsch the department's approval of his position.[6] The action was significant in that Reinsch felt free to devise new forays against Japanese pretensions.

These were not long in the making. By February, 1917, Reinsch had come forward with a plan to link the United States and China with an alliance. While details were not developed, the general character of the scheme may be stated. The United States would provide China with economic aid and give firm guarantees of China's independence. This would rescue China from the dangers of Japanese conquest. Benefits would accrue to the United States in the form of assurances that the vast manpower and resources of China would never be used against Americans. To Reinsch, the need for such an arrangement was apparent. The record of quarrels between the United States and Japan since 1907 made war all too likely a possibility. Japanese expansion was seen as part of a program to obtain for Japan control of men and supplies for the struggle. By linking her fortunes with China then, the United States would discharge her moral duty and provide for her own defense.

Like the suggested joint railway project, this scheme was improvised without reference to the State Department. The occasion was Wilson's blanket invitation to neutral nations to follow the American lead in severing diplomatic relations with Germany. Wilson apparently did not expect his invitation to be interpreted literally. He hoped neutrals would respond by censuring Germany's return to unrestricted submarine warfare. But Reinsch perceived in the invitation an opportunity to form a close association between the United States and China. Within hours after receiving a transcript of the President's message, Reinsch was offering Chinese officials his proposition in return

[5] Reinsch to Lansing, Jan. 30, 1917, *For. Rels., 1917*, p. 171.
[6] Polk (for Lansing) to Reinsch, Feb. 13, 1917, *For. Rels., 1917*, p. 175.

for a break in relations between China and Germany. Tuan Chi-jui, the war lord then serving as Premier, drove a hard bargain. Certain that Reinsch's scheme would be resented in Tokyo, he asked for specific guarantees that the United States would safeguard China's military establishment and general administration from Japanese retaliation. He also requested promises of American support for Chinese aims at the general peace conference.[7] Reinsch, anxious to close the deal before the Japanese heard about it, stated his personal conviction that the American government would satisfy the Chinese desires.[8] Only after stating this view did the Minister inform Washington of what he had done.

Lansing and Wilson were alarmed by the Minister's action. They agreed that the plan would be interpreted in Tokyo as an attempt to eliminate Japanese influence in China. Japan would certainly not allow the move to go unchallenged. Since the United States was unprepared to cope with the measures Japan would undoubtedly use, the only course was to disassociate the American government from the scheme as gracefully as possible.[9] China was informed that Reinsch's statements did not have official sanction.[10] The Minister was reprimanded in a sharply worded cable which advised the utmost caution "lest China through our advice should become involved in difficulties from which we shall be unable to extricate it."[11]

The damage, however, could not be repaired. Late in February Japan, having no certain knowledge of the individual character of Reinsch's proposal, urged Peking to associate itself with Tokyo in making the break with Germany. Large loans,

[7] Reinsch to Lansing, Feb. 6, 1917 (two telegrams), *For. Rels., 1917, Supp. 1,* (Washington, 1931), 401-402.

[8] Reinsch to Lansing, Feb. 7, 8, 1917, *For. Rels., 1917, Supp. 1,* pp. 403-404.

[9] Wilson to Lansing, Feb. 9; Lansing to Wilson, Feb. 10, 1917, SD 763.72/3275 1/2, 3275.

[10] Lansing to Reinsch, Feb. 10, 1917 (two telegrams), *For. Rels., 1917,* p. 408.

[11] Lansing to Reinsch, Feb. 26, 1917, *For. Rels., 1917, Supp. 1,* p. 411.

unencumbered by demands for collateral, were offered in return for the favor. Clearly Japan was preparing to outbid the United States for China's friendship.[12] Chinese officials, who were alert to opportunities to advance their personal fortunes and power, were quick to perceive the possibilities of this situation. They sought to induce the United States, Japan, Britain, and France to bid against each other for China's entry into the war. This was a dangerous game. Japan's response might be a precipitous move to impose new limits on China's independence. Quite unwittingly Reinsch had contributed to China's perils.

The climax to these events needs only to be sketched here. On March 14 the Peking regime, following Japan's lead, broke diplomatic relations with Germany. Tuan's opponents, fearing the consolidation of the Premier's rule as a result of war loans to his regime, started a revolution which lasted into the summer of 1917. Out of the welter Tuan emerged triumphant in July. The restoration of Tuan to the Premiership was in no small measure due to Japanese assistance. That the regime was pro-Japanese in its orientation was demonstrated soon after Tuan resumed office. Japanese banks loaned Peking Yen 10,000,000 and made representations to the powers on behalf of China asking postponement of the Boxer Rebellion indemnity payments and increases in the Chinese tariff.

Lansing watched these developments with increasing discomfiture. He anticipated that the spread of internal disorder would increase opportunities for Japanese encroachment on China's sovereignty. Consequently, he attempted to calm the Chinese. The day before China broke with Germany Lansing advised Peking that the United States would not protect China against efforts (presumably coming from Japan) to seize her military establishment.[13] When this failed to accomplish anything, the Secretary sought to organize the powers to make a joint representation to China. The powers would urge China

[12] Reinsch to Lansing, Feb. 28, 1917, *For. Rels., 1917, Supp. 1,* p. 412.
[13] Lansing to Reinsch, March 13, 1917, *For. Rels., 1917, Supp. 1,* pp. 419-420.

to abandon consideration of entry into the war and to exert her energies toward the establishment of domestic harmony.[14] This was intended to discourage further Chinese efforts to play the powers against each other. But the maneuver misfired. After indicating approval of the idea, Japan withdrew from the project.[15] The United States sent the note independently on June 4, 1917, an act which seemed to have no effect on events in China. It did, however, arouse intense public criticism of the United States in Japan. Americans were accused of attempting to influence the Chinese against Japan.[16] Following this failure, Lansing ceased further efforts to influence Tuan through diplomatic representations. No effort was made to block the Japanese loan. Nor did Lansing oppose the entry of China into the war under Japanese auspices in August. Privately, he deplored these events, but he felt anything the United States might do would probably result in the strengthening of ties between Peking and Tokyo.[17]

By the end of the summer of 1917 it was apparent that Reinsch's efforts to aid China and align her with the United States had brought unwelcome results. The disinclination of the Wilson administration to go beyond the use of peaceful means in assisting China and disorder within China itself wrecked the Minister's plans. Instead of drawing closer to the United States the Peking regime moved decidedly into the Japanese camp. The events effecting this change brought still another consequence: Japan's anxieties concerning American intentions were magnified by sharp turns in policy. Against Lansing's assurance that the United States did not challenge Japan's "special interests" in South Manchuria, Japan set Reinsch's proposed joint railway enterprise, his effort to purchase a Chinese break with Germany, and the State Department's efforts to keep China

[14] Lansing to Reinsch, June 4, 1917, *For. Rels., 1917,* p. 48.

[15] The Japanese Ambassador in Washington apparently approved the idea without first consulting his government. Lansing, *War Memoirs,* p. 287.

[16] Wheeler to Lansing, June 1, 9, 1917, *For. Rels., 1917,* pp. 48, 58.

[17] Polk to Reinsch, Aug. 4, 1917, *For. Rels., 1917,* pp. 89-90. Lansing to Reinsch, Aug. 14, 1917, *For. Rels., 1917, Supp. 1,* p. 456.

out of the war after Japan had begun to urge that step on Peking. These moves, especially when they were viewed in the context of increased American activity in China, encouraged Japan to suspect the worst. Not only did the United States appear to be launching an attack on Japan's spheres of influence, but she also seemed to be trying to turn China against Japan. Out of these deepening suspicions came the Japanese motive for seeking discussions with the American government. Lansing's remarks to the Japanese Ambassador on January 25 provided an opening, into which the Japanese moved.

What the American position in these talks would be was not clear. Reinsch's moves evoked divergent responses in Washington. Lansing had raised his proposed bargain and had received Wilson's sanction. But it appears that the President was not firmly committed to the idea. Reinsch's protests against Lansing's remarks to the Japanese Ambassador and Polk's subsequent approval of the joint railway suggestion point to the absence of an agreed American policy. This uncertainty was to continue through the beginning of the Lansing-Ishii talks. An explanation of this situation must be given. It will indicate the methods used by Lansing in pressing for a settlement with Japan.

The vagueness in administration policy was related to Lansing's working arrangements with the President. By early 1917 the friction which was to lead to an open break between the two men was beginning to appear. Wilson complained that Lansing was the most unsatisfactory Secretary in the Cabinet. Lansing possessed "no imagination, no constructive ability, and but little real ability of any kind."[18] The source of irritation seems to have been Lansing's practice of urging steps which were distasteful to the President. For example, Lansing, who was convinced that the United States must soon enter the war against Germany, remarked to newspaper reporters in December, 1916, that the United States might be forced into war. The

[18] March 28, 1917, House Diary.

comment was made deliberately. It was part of Lansing's program to educate Wilson and the American populace about the necessities of the time.[19] Since the remark cast doubt on Wilson's own effort to keep the country neutral, the President angrily ordered a retraction. Lansing complied, but according to Mrs. Wilson, the incident caused the President to have grave doubts about the soundness of Lansing's judgment.[20]

Lansing's knowledge of the President's mental processes enabled him to sense Wilson's mood. Personally he was offended by Wilson's reaction to his work. He was especially irked by Wilson's growing tendency to ignore him when decisions were to be made on policy questions. He complained to House, who noted that "Lansing seldom sees the President, and as far as he is concerned, the State Department is sailing without a chart."[21] He did not permit these feelings, however, to blur his judgment in choosing the tactics which he employed for achieving his aims. As long as Wilson was incensed with Lansing, it seemed unwise for the Secretary to approach the President directly about striking a bargain with Japan. Wilson's peevishness might influence him against the scheme. In the circumstances, it seemed advisable to allow the question to go unanswered a while longer. Wilson's response to Lansing's account of his January 25 conversation with the Japanese Ambassador suggested that in time the President might come around to support the idea.

[19] Lansing, *War Memoirs,* p. 23.

[20] E. B. Wilson, *Memoirs,* pp. 123-126. Also see Dec. 21, 1916, House Diary.

[21] Jan. 4, 1917, House Diary. Lansing told Polk that "He saw more of [Arthur] Balfour, during the few weeks he was here, than he has seen of the President in six months."—May 30, 1917, House Diary. This was a fairly common complaint of Cabinet members. Aug. 15, 1917, House Diary.

9. The Bargain Evaporates

Japan's request for talks came on May 12, 1917. The United States had entered the war and was preparing to receive European commissions to discuss co-ordination of war efforts. Tokyo asked if she might send a delegation to talk about the war, Japanese immigration, loans to China, and other Far Eastern matters.[1] To this request Lansing gave an affirmative reply. The United States, he added, preferred not to draw up an agenda in advance. This should be left open until discussions were started.[2] The way was thus cleared for the famed negotiations which began in late summer. During the interim, both sides engaged in maneuvers which suggest what they hoped to achieve at the meeting.

The American reasons for agreeing to talks were as pressing as those prompting Japan to ask for them. While the country's involvement in war weakened its bargaining position in the Far East, the war itself provided the necessity for reaching an understanding with Japan. As early as 1915, the State Department began to suspect that Japan might withdraw from the alliance with Britain and France and join Germany. The suspicion was based on scattered bits of intelligence. In April, 1915, an Austrian official had approached the Japanese Ambassador in Sweden with an offer to make peace.[3] Subsequently, American

[1] Japanese Ambassador to Lansing, SD 763.72/4677 1/2.

[2] To the Japanese Ambassador, May 15, 1917, SD 763.72/4677 1/2.

[3] Bryan to Wilson, April 26, 1915, Bryan-Wilson Cor.

sources reported the transmission of large numbers of cables between Germany and Japan. These events coincided with a notable decline in popular enthusiasm in Japan for the war.[4] Evidence of this kind continued to accumulate, and as the United States became increasingly involved in European troubles, State Department concern mounted. The disclosure in February, 1917, of the Zimmermann Telegram, which proposed engagements among Germany, Mexico, and Japan, shook the composure of American officials. A large measure of Wilson's and Lansing's concern over Reinsch's unauthorized moves in Peking was related to evidence of a linking of Japan and Germany. Both men thought that the Minister's action might be the very thing to precipitate the move.[5] In this sense then, the upcoming talks were regarded from the outset as a war measure. An effort would be made to compose Japanese-American differences so that there would be no impediment to the fight against the Central Powers.

But how were these differences to be composed? Conflicts between the two nations sprang from several sources. China was the central problem, but there was also the question of American treatment of Japanese immigrants. Past failures to achieve understandings cast doubt on the value of the impending conversations. In the midst of war would the United States and Japan be flexible enough to achieve agreement?

[4] Polk Memorandum, Dec. 15, 1915, Polk Papers.

[5] In a memorandum for Lansing, Williams pointed out the consequence of supporting Reinsch's proposed Sino-American alliance: "We are thus brought face to face with the possibility that Japan may join the Germans against us if we interfere in China. Such an occasion would mean further aggression by Japan upon China's sovereignty and territorial integrity, if not the complete conquest of China.

"If we can prevent Japan's defection and at the same time build up China's military organization, we should not only do a great service to China but preserve our own interests in the Far East, but if Japan should get control of China's military establishment she would become a menace to western civilization.

"Matters have gone so far that if we are not prepared to risk Japan's opposition, we should either have a frank understanding with Japan . . . , or repudiate Minister Reinsch's agreement."—Feb. 14, 1917, Long Papers, "China, Military Loan."

Lansing thought so. During the summer of 1916, Ambassador George Guthrie had written the Secretary private letters from Tokyo. These emphasized the growing influence of businessmen and financiers in Japanese politics. The net result had been the strengthening of Japan's desire to make a firm settlement of all problems with the United States. The business world had a clearer notion than most Japanese of the extent to which Japan's own economic growth depended upon the development of commercial ties with the United States.[6] This thesis was supported by information from other sources. For example, Lansing learned that certain Japanese officials believed that American armed forces would be turned against Japan as soon as the European war ended.[7] According to these Japanese, such an event must be avoided. Not only would Japan's economy be destroyed, but Japan probably would lose the fight.[8] Finally, the Secretary knew that a settlement was attractive to the Terauchi Ministry for reasons which grew out of the Ministry's struggle to remain in power. Since taking office, the Terauchi government had pursued a policy of ostensible noninterference in Chinese affairs. This policy made the Ministry vulnerable to attack by extremists urging a strong line of action. Japanese opinion was particularly sensitive to any American moves which seemed to curtail Japan's opportunity in China. The Cabinet reasoned that an understanding with the United States would quiet this source of opposition.[9] From such evidence Lansing concluded that there was a peace party in Japan. Moreover, it seemed clear that this group was prepared to make concessions to the United States.

Guthrie's talks with Japanese officials revealed what these

[6] Aug. 1; Sept. 25, 1916, SD 793.94/538 1/2, 540 1/2.

[7] Lansing, *War Memoirs,* p. 285.

[8] William Phillips to Polk (reporting substance of a conversation between the British and Japanese Ambassadors in Washington), Feb. 17, 1917, Polk Papers. The British government was concerned by American-Japanese difficulties. During 1917 British diplomats sought to bring about an understanding. The report of the conversation just noted was typical of British activities.

[9] Wheeler to Lansing, June 14, 1917, *For. Rels., 1917,* pp. 68-69.

might be. Japan would probably make no complaint about any American disposition of the immigrant question. She was likely to surrender her claims to Germany's political and military rights in Shantung. Finally, the establishment of American commercial interests in China Proper would not be resisted, if the United States did not make exclusive claims. In return Japan would insist on a clear understanding on China. Japan was deeply concerned by the apparent vacillation of America's China policy. She desired firm assurances on two points: the United States must formally recognize the existence of Japan's "special interests" in South Manchuria; the American government must also pledge not to engage in any attempt to deprive Japan of her leadership in East Asia.[10]

Confirmation of the official character of these views came in July, 1917. Nicholas Murray Butler, then President of the Carnegie Endowment for International Peace, transmitted to Lansing a letter giving the substance of an interview between a certain Mr. Miyaoka, a Carnegie official, and Viscount Ichiro Motono, Japan's Minister of Foreign Affairs. The interview lasted for more than two hours, during which time Motono expressed himself in detail concerning American-Japanese relations. Since the Minister was told in advance that his views would be sent to "friends" in America, Motono presumably intended to convey his thoughts to the State Department. He was not to be disappointed. Lansing read the letter along with a number of other documents bearing on possible Japanese concessions which he had pulled from the files.

Motono's formula for settling outstanding difficulties distinguished between China Proper, on one hand, and South Manchuria and Eastern Inner Mongolia, on the other. China Proper could be regarded as a neutral market where all nations might compete for commercial advantage. The other areas would stand on different planes. In those, Japan would insist on

[10] Guthrie to Lansing, Aug. 1; Sept. 5, 25, 1916; Jan. 18, 1917, SD 793.94/538 1/2, 539 1/2, 540 1/2, 573.

the exclusive right to make investments and carry on all the other activities that had come to be associated with a sphere of influence. Japan would give specific guarantees that she would not seek monopoly in China Proper or interfere in domestic politics there in return for American recognition of Japan's claims. Furthermore, Japan would promise not to raise again the troublesome question of immigration.[11]

Even as Lansing was collecting evidence of this kind, however, he was obliged to recognize that these Japanese concessions were not certain. On June 15, while talking to Lansing about other matters, the Japanese Ambassador, Amaro Sato, quite unexpectedly asked for reaffirmation of certain principles enumerated in the March 13, 1915, Note, especially recognition that "Japan has special and close relations, political as well as economic with China. . . ."[12] This was a clever move. In making the request the Ambassador made two important changes in phraseology. One was to define the phrase "special interests," for which no definition was given in the American Note, as meaning "political" and "economic" relations. The second change was to claim American willingness to recognize Japan's "special interests" in *all* of China, whereas the Note had specified only Shantung, South Manchuria, and Eastern Inner Mongolia. Lansing, who was quite unprepared for the request, failed to note the changes and stated orally his "accord with the deep sense of the memorandum."[13]

A few days later the American Chargé d'Affaires in Tokyo was handed a document that was purported to be the text of the request made of Lansing. The language, however, was varied again. The line quoted above was now made to read, "Japan possessed paramount interests both political and economic in

[11] T. Miyaoka to Butler, June 12, 1917. Forwarded to Lansing, July 10, SD 793.94/587 1/2.

[12] Sato to Lansing, *For. Rels., 1917*, p. 259.

[13] Wheeler to Lansing, June 18, 1917, *For. Rels., 1917*, p. 259. The Department had been warned that such an attempt might be forthcoming, but the notice had apparently not reached Lansing. Wheeler to Lansing, June 4, 1917, *For. Rels., 1917*, pp. 68-71.

China."[14] The effect of this change was to make "special and close relations" synonymous with "paramount interests."[15] As a final step, the Foreign Office expressed to Lansing its "deep sense of gratitude" for his reply.[16]

Japan's purpose was to improve her bargaining position. By committing the United States to a broad construction of her "special interests," Japan would be able to press for American recognition of her leadership in East Asia. For instance, Japan might ask the United States to refrain from political activities in China without first consulting Japan.[17] But the maneuver failed. After comparing the texts of the various memoranda, Lansing informed Sato that his oral statement was intended, "to vary in no way the formal declaration of Mr. Bryan." The United States had referred to the existence of Japan's "special interests" only in certain regions. Moreover, the term "special interests" had never been defined in the ways Japan contended.[18] The record now stood exactly where it had been.

The importance of Japan's démarche was that it emphasized to Lansing the precarious position of Japanese officials who were seeking a settlement with the United States. In June the State Department learned of the reaction to Lansing's note of the fourth to Peking. This note contained the plea to China to remain out of the war and mend her internal divisions. Opponents of the Terauchi Ministry had used this advice to stir up public opinion. The United States was charged with seeking to control China's foreign policy. The Ministry, it was claimed,

[14] Wheeler to Lansing, June 22, 1917, *Lansing Papers,* II, 430.

[15] Lansing, *War Memoirs,* p. 289.

[16] Lansing to Reinsch (quoting the Japanese note), June 29, 1917, *For. Rels., 1917,* p. 78.

[17] There is no doubt that this was the aim of certain Japanese. On Oct. 22, 1917, the Russian Ambassador in Tokyo cabled St. Petersburg: "The Japanese are manifesting more and more clearly a tendency to interpret the special position of Japan in China, *inter alia,* in the sense that other Powers must not undertake in China any political steps without previously exchanging views with Japan on the subject."—Printed in F. Seymour Cocks, ed., *The Secret Treaties and Understandings* (London, 1918), p. 88.

[18] Lansing to Sato, July 6, 1917, *For. Rels., 1917,* pp. 260-262.

was doing nothing to block the accomplishment of the American aim. The charge touched a popular chord. All over the country a clamor was raised. From this, the American Chargé concluded that proponents of conciliation would have a hard time staying in office.[19] Subsequent research tends to support this observation. Viscount Motono, who seems to have taken the lead in urging a settlement, had the double liability of being an advocate of potentially unpopular views and having little political strength. A career diplomat, Motono had spent much of his life in France. He had become a cultured European and had married a French woman. It was asserted that his French was better than his Japanese. Certainly he understood European politics better than those in Japan. The result was that he tended to be isolated in the Cabinet.[20] In retrospect it is clear that any hope of obtaining Japanese concessions rested on America's willingness to reciprocate in such measure as to enable Japanese politicians to demonstrate publicly some real accomplishment on their part.

While the delicate balances within the Japanese government were partly concealed from the State Department, Lansing sensed the significance of the events just outlined. As soon as it was known that a Japanese mission was coming to Washington, he began to press once again for a bargain. He did not do this directly, for the President's attitude did not seem to make that course feasible. Colonel House provided a better channel. House was fond of Lansing and frequently sought out the Secretary for talks on foreign affairs. From these contacts Lansing discovered House's mind to be like a sponge. House absorbed information and ideas and quickly made them his own. Soon he was presenting them to the President as products of his own thought. A man with a temperament different from Lansing's would have resented the practice intensely. But until the time of the Peace Conference Lansing displayed no irritation.[21]

[19] Wheeler to Lansing, June 14, 1917, *For. Rels., 1917*, pp. 68-69.

[20] James W. Morley, *The Japanese Thrust into Siberia, 1918* (New York, 1957), p. 54. Hereinafter cited as Morley, *Japanese Thrust*.

[21] Mrs. Wilson took House aside early in 1917 to tell him a story then

Rather, he turned the situation to own purposes. He used House to convey to Wilson programs which might be unacceptable coming from himself.

Lansing worked on House through the spring and early summer. The two men had long conferences and some correspondence about Japan. In these contacts Lansing hammered on ideas which he had first advanced during the Twenty-one Demands crisis. To these ideas he added one new point: the United States should transfer control of the Philippines to Japan. Apparently Lansing felt that the colonial status of these islands weakened America's hand in dealing with Japan by casting doubt on the frequent assertion that the United States had no political interests in the Orient.[22] House agreed with most of what Lansing told him.[23] In August and September—just as the Lansing-Ishii talks were starting—House began to urge Wilson to make the desired concessions.[24]

While the maneuvering just described was occurring, the State Department made detailed plans for the reception of the Japanese. Particular attention was given to entertainment. Elaborate dinners, formal receptions, and tours of various cities were scheduled. The Washington mansion belonging to Perry Belmont, who was the grandson of Commodore Matthew Perry, was obtained to house the Ishii Mission. To lessen the chance of hostile demonstrations while Ishii was in the country, the press was requested to refrain from speculating about the purpose of the negotiation or discussing differences between the

current in Washington. This concerned a "new" way of spelling "Lansing." This was "H-O-U-S-E." The Colonel assured Mrs. Wilson that such stories had no effect on Lansing. He added, "Lansing is a pretty big fellow in that way and does not seem to be disturbed by jealousy."—March 3, 1917, House Diary. Also see the Diary entry for Sept. 13, 1917.

[22] This was not a new idea with Lansing. He had mentioned it to House on July 24, 1915. House Diary.

[23] March 24; April 29, 1917, House Diary. House to Lansing, June 27, 1917. House Papers, House to Lansing File.

[24] Aug. 4; Sept. 6; Sept. 18, 1917, House Diary. House to Wilson, Sept. 18, 1917, Wilson Papers, II, 126.

United States and Japan.[25] Much time was expended preparing for the talks themselves. Biographical data were collected on each member of the Mission. Department files were combed for clues as to what the Japanese would discuss. All of these activities were supervised closely by Lansing. The Secretary noted that an unusual amount of work was going into the receiving of the Japanese, but he felt the effort worthwhile. To House he confided that the Ishii Mission was "as important as any which has visited us and requires very careful handling."[26]

The Ishii Mission, which consisted of eight representatives of the Foreign Office, Army, and Navy, arrived in San Francisco on August 13. After being feted by the city and reviewing a contingent of American troops, the emissaries traveled across the country in a chartered train.[27] In Washington they were swept into a round of parties and receptions. Ishii was invited to speak before Congress. At Lansing's suggestion, the entire delegation reviewed the Atlantic fleet.[28] Since these preliminaries filled the days, no talks were held until the first week in September. When negotiations started, they proceeded on two separate levels. Military representatives discussed co-ordination of the war effort while Lansing and Ishii took up political questions. Of the talks, only the political ones had lasting significance. Japan was by that time playing a relatively insignificant role in the war. In consequence, military discussions were held to minor matters.[29]

[25] David Lawrence to Oswald Garrison Villard, Aug. 2, 1917. Quoted in Daniel J. Gage, "Paul S. Reinsch and Sino-American Relations" (unpublished doctoral dissertation, Stanford University, 1939), p. 660.

[26] Lansing to House, June 8, 1917, House Papers, "Lansing to House File." Lansing wrote the same thing to the President. June 10, 1917, Wilson Papers, II, 120. Twenty-five thousand dollars was allotted for entertainment alone.

[27] Breckinridge Long, who met the Mission in San Francisco, later recalled that every soldier on the West Coast was put into the parade.

[28] Lansing to Daniels; Daniels to Lansing, Aug. 14, 16, 1917, The Library of Congress, The Papers of Josephus Daniels, "Correspondence, Navy Period, Lansing File."

[29] It was agreed to replace the American cruiser, *Saratoga,* which was in Hawaiian waters, with a Japanese vessel. Talks were opened on the exchange of American steel for Japanese shipping.

Political talks began on September 5. The burden of the negotiations fell on Lansing and Ishii, but the documents eventually signed by these men did not reflect their own views. Both men worked under close supervision. Ishii arrived in Washington without definitive instructions. In consequence, negotiations were sometimes delayed while Tokyo was consulted. Lansing followed Wilson's directives, and, indeed, on two occasions stepped aside so that Ishii might talk directly to the President.

Negotiations opened with a conversation between Wilson and Ishii. Prior to this House had asked Wilson to give Japan a sympathetic hearing.[30] While the talks were in progress, he outlined to the President the idea of a bargain with Japan.[31] Wilson, however, was unimpressed. Speaking to Ishii, he outlined the position that he was to hold throughout the negotiations. Japan was asked to pledge to observe faithfully the principles of the Open Door and equal opportunity for all nations in China. In effect, he asked Japan to renounce her claims to "special interests" in the Chinese Empire and to bind herself not to reassert such claims in the future.[32] Wilson had not changed his mind since 1915. Japanese encroachments on China's integrity, the President held, were violations of high moral principle. It was, therefore, America's continuing duty to safeguard China from this foreign danger.

Wilson's remarks indicated clearly to Ishii the gulf between the United States and Japan. Ishii was instructed to obtain American pledges on two things: the United States must guarantee that she would not attempt to influence China against Japan

[30] Aug. 4, 1917, House Diary.

[31] House told Roland S. Morris, newly appointed Ambassador to Japan, of his idea before Morris went to talk with Wilson. The interview was followed by a letter to Wilson suggesting that the President might wish to instruct Morris along the line indicated. Sept. 18, 1917, House Diary. House to Wilson, Sept. 18, 1917, Wilson Papers, II, 126.

[32] Kikujiro Ishii, *Diplomatic Commentaries,* translated and edited by William R. Langdon (Baltimore, 1936), p. 112. Hereinafter cited as Ishii, *Commentaries.*

or challenge Japan's "special interests" in South Manchuria and Eastern Inner Mongolia. In discussing the unsettled immigration dispute, Ishii was to seek a treaty which would guarantee to Japanese living in the United States a status equal to that of other aliens. Japan was prepared to offer in return for these concessions assurances that she would not monopolize business opportunities in China Proper and would permit Americans to co-operate with Japanese firms in ventures carried on within Japan's spheres of influence.[33] From these instructions it is clear that Ishii had come to the United States hoping to achieve a genuine settlement. The instructions paralleled the terms outlined by Motono two months earlier, and the Japanese Foreign Minister, as has been shown, was then seeking to demonstrate Japan's readiness to accept the bargain which had been proposed by the United States. Ishii must have been disappointed to find Wilson as unyielding as ever.

Nor can it be assumed that disappointment was confined to the Japanese emissary. Lansing had reason to think that Ishii carried with him the terms which Motono had outlined. Ishii's appointment as head of the Japanese Mission was one indication of this. The career diplomat, widely respected in Tokyo, was reputed to be friendly toward the United States. The State Department interpreted the appointment as an indication that Japan intended its Mission to deal in more than formalities.[34] But it was also clear that Ishii was not free to make the settlement Wilson wanted. The necessity for American recognition of Japan's "special interests" was underlined by the dispatch of 50,000 Japanese troops to South Manchuria between June and August of 1917 and by Motono's reiteration on the eve of Ishii's departure for the United States of the terms which would be acceptable to the Terauchi Ministry.[35] Thus, almost from the

[33] Hikomatsu Kamikawa, ed., *Japan-American Diplomatic Relations in the Meiji-Taisho Era,* translated by Michiko Kimura (Tokyo, 1958), pp. 339-342.

[34] Roland S. Morris, "The Memoirs of Viscount Ishii," *Foreign Affairs,* X (July, 1932), 677-678. "Report of the Personnel of the Extraordinary Japanese Mission," SD 763.72/13441.

[35] Long Memorandum, July 10, 1917, Long Papers, "Memoranda, Japan,

outset Lansing suspected that his hopes for a bargain were doomed. Yet there was little he could do about it. His relations with Wilson continued to be bad. Even as Lansing was holding his first talks with Ishii, Wilson was thinking of asking for the Secretary's resignation. According to House, only his own exertions prevented the step.[36] In the circumstances Lansing had little choice other than to follow Wilson's lead while hoping for a miraculous change in Wilson's thinking or Japanese policy.

In a session with Ishii on September 6, Lansing argued the President's case. The advantages of renouncing claims to spheres of influence were pointed out. On one hand, Britain, France, and the United States would be encouraged to press the fight in Europe by this sign of Japan's unselfishness. On the other, Japan would lose nothing by such renunciation. Japan's geographic position provided her with natural advantages over other nations in developing commercial relations with China. And finally, Japan should recognize that her prestige among nations would rise as a result of her fair dealing with China.[37] Lansing's experience as a lawyer served him well in advancing these arguments. A skilled advocate, he gave no sign that he was not presenting his own view. Indeed, Ishii later recalled that the Secretary's extreme "pro-Chinese" tendencies presented a major obstacle to the achievement of an understanding.[38]

Following these initial conversations, the negotiators stalled while Ishii cabled for instructions. The delay raised American hopes that Japan might be preparing to accept the conditions laid down by Wilson. Later Ishii, writing in his memoirs, ad-

1917-1918." Long Memorandum, Oct. 27, 1917, Long Papers, "China, Military Loan." While talks were continuing in October, Kataro Mochizuki, member of the Japanese Parliamentary Commission then visiting the United States and an outspoken foe of Ishii and the Terauchi Ministry, visited the State Department to emphasize the necessity of American recognition of Japan's "special interests." Long Memorandum, Oct. 24, 1917, Long Papers, "Memoranda, Japan, 1917-1918."

[36] Sept. 9, 10, 12, 1917, House Diary.

[37] For detailed accounts see Lansing Memoranda, *Lansing Papers,* II, 432-434. Lansing, *War Memoirs,* p. 293; Ishii, *Commentaries,* pp. 115-117.

[38] Ishii, *Commentaries,* p. 122.

mitted that he did urge the American view on Tokyo. Lansing was correct, he held, in saying that Japan's dominance in the development of commercial interests in China did not rest on monopolistic claims. By September 22, however, he abandoned his effort to convert the Ministry. In a statement to Lansing, he said flatly that Japan would not renounce her claims. The uncompromising nature of the statement reflected the fact that the Foreign Affairs Investigation Council, then the supreme body in matters of foreign policy, had refused to approve Ishii's recommendation.[39]

The Japanese action came at a crucial moment. Four days earlier House made his final effort to persuade Wilson to make concessions. By September 24 Lansing knew the effort had failed.[40] Both sides had stated their positions and remained far apart. It was unlikely that the deadlock could be resolved.

Recognition of this did not result in the breaking off of negotiations. Popular attention in Japan was focused on the Ishii Mission. The Japanese generally assumed that the negotiations would materially advance the nation's interest.[41] Lansing was cognizant of this feeling and wished to avoid the appearance of failure. If an offense to Japanese sensibilities were committed, the Terauchi Ministry would come under fire from extremists. Ishii had hinted darkly what the result might be: a stronger China policy and Japan's defection from her alliances.[42] Lansing needed no reminders on either score. As has been noted, he knew enough about Japan's internal affairs to regard these things as distinct possibilities. Now that negotiations were started the diplomats were obliged to produce evidence of harmony.

[39] Ishii, *Commentaries,* pp. 114-115.

[40] On the twenty-fourth Wilson saw Morris, whom House had urged be instructed along the lines of his letter of Sept. 18. Wilson, however, failed to give Morris any instructions. "Memorandum of Ray Stannard Baker Interview with Roland S. Morris," March 7, 8, 1926. Baker Papers, I, 45, Morris File. The episode provided Lansing with an indication of Wilson's thinking.

[41] Wheeler to Lansing, June 29, 1917, SD 763.72/5998.

[42] Lansing Memoranda, Sept. 6, 22, 1917, *Lansing Papers,* II, 432-437.

To do this Lansing resorted to ambiguity. On September 26 he proposed issuing a joint declaration in which the United States would recognize Japan's "special interests" in return for Japanese adherence to the following statement:

The Governments of the United States and Japan deny that they have any purpose to infringe in any way the independence or territorial integrity of China and they declare furthermore that they always adhere to the principle of the so-called Open Door or equal opportunity for commerce and industry in China, and that they will not take advantage of present conditions to seek special rights and privileges in China which would abridge the rights of the citizens or subjects of other friendly states. Moreover, they mutually declare that they are opposed to the acquisition by any other government of special rights or privileges that would affect the independence or territorial integrity of China or that would deny to the subjects or citizens of any country the full enjoyment of equal opportunity in the commerce and industry of China.[43]

The formula did not provide a solution for American-Japanese differences. American recognition of Japan's "special interests" gave the latter nation an opening for pressing her claims. The joint declaration pledging observance of the Open Door and equal opportunity served the same purpose as the Bryan-Lansing caveat of May, 1915: it provided an American reservation with regard to future Japanese action. In effect, Lansing suggested simply a declaration of divergent aims which was phrased to make it appear that agreement had been achieved.[44] Ishii indicated his willingness to accept the idea.[45]

From this point negotiations dealt mainly with the language to be used to express the formula. Ishii undertook to substitute "paramount interests" for "special interests" and urged the omis-

[43] *Lansing Papers,* II, 440-441.

[44] Williams, who drafted the declaration, recalled the fine shades of meaning attached to the wording. Japan claimed that the Notes recognized her "special interests" in Shantung. The United States, however, could argue that Japan was not "contiguous" to Shantung; she only enjoyed "propinquity." Edward T. Williams, "Japan's Interests in Manchuria," *University of California Chronicle,* XXIV (Jan., 1932), 17-19.

[45] Lansing Memorandum, Sept. 26, 1917, *Lansing Papers,* II, 438.

sion of the portion of the declaration pertaining to the use of the war to upset the status quo. These changes would narrow the grounds for America's seeking redress at some future date. Lansing parried the effort. "Special interests" remained the phrase to express Japan's relations to China. The second Japanese objection was resolved by adopting a secret protocol which contained the substance of the pledge quoted above.[46] In the final draft of the public notes, the United States recognized that "territorial propinquity creates special relations between countries and, consequently, the Government of the United States recognizes that Japan has special interests in China, especially the part to which her possessions are contiguous." Japan went on record in a long declaration of respect for the Open Door and the independence and integrity of China. Lansing and Ishii affixed their signatures to the completed documents on November 2, 1917.[47]

What had been accomplished by these negotiations? Certainly they had not worked out the way Lansing had hoped. The bargain, which Lansing thought was desirable, and which the record suggests was possible, was not made. Any achievement must be measured in terms of how well the joint declaration assisted the defense of China and the war effort.

With respect to the first of these, American officials were unanimous in claiming gains. Wilson believed that he had served China well. The pledges made by Japan would restrain that country from making further encroachments on China's independence. In public statements made at the time and in later years, Lansing supported his chief. The Secretary argued that the language of the joint declaration strengthened America's position in seeking redress from Japan. For example, the Lansing-Ishii Notes had used the phrase "special interests" to de-

[46] The secret agreement was made in the form of a joint memorandum signed by the two negotiators. It is printed in the *Lansing Papers,* II, 450-451. The record of the negotiations is printed in Lansing Memoranda, Oct. 10, 20, 22, 27, 29, 30, 1917, *Lansing Papers,* II, 441-449; Lansing, *War Memoirs,* pp. 298-300; Ishii, *Commentaries,* pp. 119-123.

[47] *For. Rels., 1917,* p. 264.

scribe Japan's relation to China instead of "special relations," which had been the term employed in the March 13, 1915, Note.[48] The value of this substitution, of course, depended on America's ability to force a showdown with Japan at some future date. As far as Japan was concerned, the change in phraseology was at the time of no great importance. The Japanese government regarded her pledge as no more binding on her action than numerous similar declarations made in the past.

While Lansing never admitted this publicly, he was aware of the Japanese intrepretation. A short time before negotiations were concluded he learned of a conversation between the Japanese Foreign Minister and Russian Ambassador in Tokyo. Japan, the Foreign Minister had said, intended to claim that American recognition of her "special interests" extended to all of China. Furthermore, Japan would interpret the phrase in the broadest sense.[49] Lansing's failure to discuss this aspect may probably be attributed to his strong sense of duty. During his lifetime, China remained an issue between the United States and Japan. A full, frank account of what he had attempted in 1917 might have contributed to contemporary estimates of his ability as a diplomat, but it could possibly have impeded the conduct of current diplomacy.

Whether American officials admitted it or not, the failure of the Lansing-Ishii Notes to impose immediate restraints on Japan was soon revealed. Late in 1917 Japan began to tighten her hold on Shantung. She established a general administrative zone along the Shantung Railway. This permitted Japanese control over the policing, taxation, forestry, and educational operations within ten miles of the railroad. In 1918 K. Nishihara

[48] Lansing, *War Memoirs,* pp. 305-306. For the fullest exposition, see "Lansing-Ishii Agreement," Oct. 3, 1921, Lansing Collection, "Private Memoranda." This memorandum was drafted while Lansing was retained as a legal adviser to the Chinese delegation at the Washington Conference.

[49] Long Memorandum, Oct. 25, 1917, SD 793.94/609. John V. A. MacMurray Memorandum, July 9, 1921, SD 793.94/609. Ishii maintained that Lansing understood the Japanese pledges to be less restrictive than he claimed. Ishii, *Commentaries,* pp. 125-128.

negotiated his famous loans with China. Through these transactions Peking exchanged concessions for cash. Japan justified these moves by referring to the language of the Lansing-Ishii Notes. The accelerated pace of Japanese activities in China suggests a weakening of the influence of moderates within the Japanese government. Officials such as Motono appear to have relied on a firm agreement with the United States to help them control their more militant colleagues. The ambiguity of the Lansing-Ishii Notes appears to have encouraged some of the more imperially minded officials to insist on steps leading to immediate fulfillment of their dreams. These factors give added weight to the point that the interests of the United States and those of China would have been better served if Wilson had attempted to strike the bargain suggested originally by Lansing and endorsed by Motono. Certainly it does not appear that such a bargain would have encouraged greater Japanese penetration of China than she undertook in the aftermath of the Lansing-Ishii negotiations, and it is possible that Japan would have abided by the bargain as Motono claimed she would.

Only as a war measure can the Lansing-Ishii Notes be accounted as a success. The Notes covered American-Japanese differences with a veneer of apparent harmony. When measured against what might have been accomplished, this seems a small gain. Yet it should not be belittled. Ishii's signature was a token of the Terauchi Ministry's attitude toward her allies: the Ministry joined in befogging current issues in order to maintain her alliances. Realization of the fact soothed Washington anxieties and facilitated concentration on the fighting which was going on in Europe. Nor should the importance of the Notes to the Far Eastern aspects of the war be overlooked. In the months ahead the United States and Japan were to grapple with complex problems which arose from the collapse of Russia's government and the Bolshevik revolution. As will be seen, the American and Japanese governments sought initially to meet these problems through the development of co-operative measures. By ending temporarily the bickering over China, the Lansing-Ishii Notes enabled the two governments to focus their attention on Siberian problems.

10. Interlude Of Co-operation

The American and Japanese determination to co-operate for the duration of the war was subjected to greater strain than either Lansing or Ishii anticipated. Before Ishii reached home Russian Bolsheviks staged their revolution. Washington and Tokyo began to consider, at first separately and then jointly, whether intervention would be advisable. By July, 1918, a decision was reached: the two powers would co-operate in sending a military expedition into Siberia. The stated purpose of the expedition was to provide assistance for Czechoslovakian troops which were fighting their way toward the Pacific coast. An opening was left, however, for conversion of the expedition to other purposes. Should the opportunity occur, troops might be used to support efforts aimed at arresting the spread of Bolshevism. Under the pressure of war and emotional stresses engendered by the spectre of world revolution, the launching of the joint expedition caused more immediate trouble between the United States and Japan than did the unsettled China questions. While the war lasted, Lansing's Far Eastern diplomacy was primarily directed at preventing the stresses of Siberian affairs from destroying the understanding reached by himself and Ishii.

Lansing's attempts to foster American-Japanese co-operation have not received much attention. America's Siberian venture has been viewed generally as another episode in the defense of the Open Door. The evidence upon which this conclusion is based may be summarized briefly. Amid the chaos ensuing in Siberia in late 1917, Japanese militarists established contacts with local Cossack leaders and sought to bring them under Japan's influence, much as had been done with the war lords in Peking. Early the following year the Japanese prepared to send an expedition into the area. To Wilson these steps meant that Japan was preparing to expand her imperial aims to include northern Manchuria and Siberia. He dispatched American troops to keep the Japanese in line. Viewed this way, the Siberian expedition was inaugurated as a continuation of the President's effort to prevent the Japanese from monopolizing East Asia.[1]

While this summary reflects the President's thought, it does not represent Lansing's. After the joint expedition had been launched, the Secretary expressed his irritation with Americans who regarded the venture as stemming from anti-Japanese considerations:

> Japanese designs as to Siberia are worrying a lot of Americans, who see in everything that the Japanese Government does some hidden motive, some insidious purpose. The present anxiety is caused by the large number of Japanese troops now in Siberia, from which it is deduced that Japan intends to annex Eastern Siberia or at least obtain all the valuable concessions in that region by bargain or threat.
>
> The Japanese are not fools. They know that a white race would never submit to the domination of a yellow race. To take the sovereignty or economic control of Eastern Siberia would mean endless trouble for Japan, as the Siberians would never rest until they had driven the Japanese out of their country.
>
> I have little patience with these people who are forever on the verge of hysterics about the deep and wicked schemes of Japan. They imagine some of the most preposterous things and report them as facts. I would think that some of these enemies of Japan were mentally unbalanced but for their sanity on all other subjects. Unfortunately they are listened to by many Americans, whose reason

[1] The best exposition of this view is Betty Miller Unterberger, *America's Siberian Expedition, 1918-1920: A Study of National Policy* (Durham, N. C., 1956). See especially pp. 87-88. See also A. Whitney Griswold, *The Far Eastern Policy of the United States* (New York, 1938), p. 234.

ought to warn them against believing such tales without better evidence.[2]

Such sentiments are scattered through Lansing's papers.[3] The Secretary's concern over Siberian affairs was aroused by reasons other than a desire to block Japan's imperial designs.

These reasons were not directly connected with the Far East. In the first place, Lansing shared the concern of his colleagues over what the Russian revolution would do to the war effort. The Bolsheviks were suspected of being German agents, and it was feared that Russia would not only be taken out of the war, but that her resources might become accessible to the Central Powers. It was with a view to finding some way of preventing these results that Lansing first turned to thoughts of intervention. Secondly, as the Bolsheviks spread over Russia, Lansing gave increasing attention to ways of destroying the revolutionaries. Lansing, who had considered Free Silver a radical idea in 1896, was appalled by the Bolshevik creed. He regarded most seriously the claims of the Reds that they were spearheading a world revolution. Between 1918 and 1920 the Secretary's books of "Private Memoranda" filled with bitter diatribes against bolshevism. The intensity of his sentiments makes scarcely surprising his tendency to look upon the joint expedition as a possible beginning in an attack on a detestable ideology.[4] In relation to these aims the Far Eastern aspects of

[2] "Suspected Designs of the Japanese in Siberia," July 31, 1919, Lansing Collection, "Private Memoranda."

[3] Shortly before his resignation, Lansing summarized his views for MacMurray, who recorded them as follows: "The Secretary said that from the beginning it had been understood that Japan contemplated no territorial acquisitions in Siberia; that they would not have sent an expedition into Siberia except in cooperation with the United States; and that such cooperation was based on the assumption that the eventual withdrawal should be complete, leaving no question of territorial enlargement; that every Japanese diplomat with whom he had ever talked had assured him that Japan had no acquisition of territory in view, and he fully believed this statement. . . ."—MacMurray to DeWitt C. Poole, Jan. 23, 1920, SD 861.00/673.

[4] Three key documents provide an outline of Lansing's evolving thought. On December 7, 1917, he discussed the possibility of secret aid to anti-Bolshevik forces. "Memorandum on the Russian Situation," Lansing Collec-

the Siberian question were secondary.

This does not mean that Lansing considered Japan's role of little consequence. Quite the contrary. Japan's geographic position gave her reason for concern at least as great as any other power over what happened in Russia. Moreover, Japan's men and resources were not committed to the European war. She was thus the only nation in a position to play a major role in Russian affairs. These factors made Japan central to any plans concerning Siberia. If Russian resources were to be denied Germany and bolshevism controlled, co-ordination of American and Japanese activities was essential. This explains Lansing's determination to prevent Siberian troubles from rupturing the understanding which had been reached with Ishii.

The events which directed Wilson's and Lansing's attention toward Siberia were set in motion by the Western Allies. Following the collapse of the Russian provisional government, Britain and France, fearing the war might yet be lost, pressed for an expedition to Russia which would be composed of Japanese forces and supplied by the United States. The expedition was initially envisaged as furnishing a guard for war material stored at Vladivostok. Later the plan was expanded to include a move west of the Ural Mountains for the purpose of re-establishing an eastern front. From December, 1917, to July, 1918, the British and French kept the question constantly before the Terauchi Ministry and Wilson administration.

The Japanese government was not united on the question. Japanese army officers, who were greatly agitated by disorders in Russia and the eastward movement of the Reds, began to argue for the dispatch of troops to Siberia as early as December, 1917. A month later they acted independently to prepare for

tion, "Private Memorandum." Less than a year later he urged Wilson to approve substantial aid for Czech and White Russian forces so that they might deal effectively with the "blood thirsty" Bolsheviks. Lansing to Wilson, Sept. 9, 1918, *Lansing Papers,* II, 381-384. At the end of 1919 Lansing submitted to Wilson an elaborate plan calling for a huge economic aid program for Russia. Its purpose was to stimulate the development of anti-Bolshevik sentiment. Lansing to Wilson, Dec. 4, 1919, Wilson Papers, II, 165.

the step. They established contacts with Russian militarists around whom they hoped a regime could be organized which would be anti-Bolshevik and pro-Japanese. These plans, however, met opposition within the Japanese government. Anti-interventionists (a coalition composed of clan leaders, bureaucrats, and party chiefs) conducted a continuing fight. These latter maintained that the situation in Russia was too unknown and the dangers of bolshevism insufficiently great to justify the sending of troops. Only if the United States approved and furnished backing for the plan, could it be considered as a practical matter. The fight, which provided a preview of later struggles within the Japanese government, was bitter and indecisive. During the first half of 1918, the opponents of intervention held control, but their hold was never secure.

There was less division within the Wilson administration. Although, as has been noted, Wilson and Lansing were to differ later in their views on the purposes of the Siberian expedition, they did not disagree when the plan was first proposed. Until June, 1918, Wilson and Lansing agreed that a military expedition was not desirable and should be avoided if possible. Two assumptions supported the conclusion. First, it was agreed that an expedition would have little effect on the war. The Russian supplies seemed in no danger of falling into German hands, and Japan's assertion that she would not send troops west of the Urals made a reactivation of the eastern front practically impossible. Second, it was believed that the expedition held dangers to American interests. President Wilson, Assistant Secretary of State Breckinridge Long, and E. T. Williams concurred in this latter assumption because they feared that Japan would use the venture to expand its claims to "special interests." Lansing was more concerned by the possibility that the expedition might lead to Japan's dropping out of the war. The Secretary suspected that a Siberian expedition might develop into a vehicle for bringing together Japanese who wished their country to defect from her alliances and German agents who were reported to be working among the Bolsheviks.[5] At this time Lansing also feared that the proposed expedition might advance the Bolshevik cause by prompting the Siberian population to rally around the Reds so as to resist forces which appeared as invaders.[6] Thus the Wilson administration rejected on no less than six occasions between January and June, 1918, formal requests for American support of a Siberian expedition.

During these months a primary problem for the Wilson administration was to keep Japan in line with the American position. Lansing sought to do this by keeping the Japanese informed about the reasons which prompted the United States to reject the proposed expedition. This strategy grew out of the State Department's awareness of the factional fight within the Japanese government. Events preceding the Lansing-Ishii talks had provided evidence of the division. More recent reports indicated that the Russian question had deepened differences among Japanese leaders. The militarists, moreover, were known to be extremely sensitive about American opposition to their plans.[7] Lansing believed they might make use of Washington's refusal to support a Siberian expedition to prove the correctness of their own contentions. The uproar precipitated by the publication of the American note asking China to stay out of the war and settle her internal troubles (June 4, 1917) illustrated how the Japanese could be aroused by a seeming affront to their national sensibilities. The episode also indicated the ways in which popular sentiment could be manipulated for the support

[5] "Memorandum on German Domination in Siberia and Possible Means of Overcoming It," March 22, 1918, Lansing Collection, "Private Memoranda." Lansing to Wilson, April 25, 29, 1918, Wilson Papers, II, 139. For evidence that Lansing was not alone in his thinking see Long to Wilson, March 4, 1918, Wilson Papers, II, 137.

[6] "Memorandum on the Proposed Japanese Expedition into Siberia," March 18, 1918, Lansing Collection, "Private Memoranda." Lansing was first warned of the danger by the Russian Ambassador in Washington. B. Bakhmetiff to Lansing, Dec. 21, 1917, Lansing Collection.

[7] Morris to Lansing, Jan. 13; Feb. 8; March 22, 1918, *For. Rels., 1918, Russia* (Washington, 1932), II, 27, 42-43, 84. Consul Morse to Lansing, April 4, 1918, Wilson Papers, II, 138.

of militant policies. Recognition of these things caused Lansing to keep in constant touch with Japanese officials. Through these contacts he sought to impress upon Japan the idea that American opposition stemmed in no way from suspicions of Japan. Such information, he hoped, would strengthen the anti-interventionists in Tokyo.

Considerable care was given to the way in which these American views were transmitted. For example, Lansing used Ishii's return to Washington as the new Japanese Ambassador as an occasion for some drama. At a ceremony in which Ishii presented his credentials to the President, Wilson, who was acting on a prior suggestion of Lansing's, quite casually asked the Ambassador to remain at the White House to discuss Russian questions. The request, which was unusual for the President to make, was designed to flatter Ishii and demonstrate the earnestness of America's desire to co-operate with Japan.[8] The content of the conversation itself was not unusual. All of the reasons making the proposed expedition inexpedient were discussed in detail; emphatic assurances were given that suspicions of Japanese aims had nothing to do with the American position. The same theme ran through virtually all of the interviews staged by the State Department with members of the Japanese Embassy staff.[9]

On only one occasion between January and June did it appear that the effort to keep Japanese troops out of Siberia would fail. In February Japan seemed ready to move. Later the appearance was discovered to have been created by Foreign Minister Motono, whose control over foreign policy had been weakened by militarists. In an effort to re-establish his authority, Motono sought unsuccessfully to make himself the leader of the interventionists. The scheme was ultimately blocked by the

[8] Lansing to Wilson, April 29, 1918, Wilson Papers, II, 139.

[9] Lansing Memorandum, Dec. 27, 1917, *For. Rels., 1918,* II, 13. Polk Memorandum, March 6, 1918, Polk Papers, Polk Diary. Lansing to Morris, March 20, 1918, SD 861.00/13605. These are examples of the contacts. Citation of all conversations would create an unnecessarily long list.

ruling coalition, and Motono was asked to resign. None of this, however, was known in Washington at the time. The assertion that Japanese troops would go to Siberia was accepted as a factual representation. The apparent firmness of Japan's decision prompted Lansing to recommend an abrupt reversal in American policy. On February 27 he departed briefly from his opposition to an expedition and urged Wilson to support the Japanese move when it materialized.[10] The reasoning behind the recommendation deserves attention because it supplies additional evidence of the factors guiding Lansing's actions.

Europe, rather than Siberia, was uppermost in Lansing's mind. British and French pleas for support of the expedition had had an upsetting effect. Lansing did not want the coalition against the Central Powers disturbed by resentment against the United States. As for Japan, there was nothing the United States could do to stop her move. It seemed sensible, then, to make the best of the situation. The British and French would be satisfied, and Japan would have no reason to complain against the United States. The powers could get on with the war. Of course, dangers remained. Japan offered to pledge publicly her intention to seek no special privilege in Siberia, but it was impossible to tell how seriously the Siberian populace would regard the profession. The possibility remained that the Japanese expedition would cause Siberians to rally around the Reds. The maintenance of harmony among the wartime partners, however, necessitated the risk. The United States, Lansing told Wilson, should be more concerned with Japanese than with Russian sensibilities.[11] Nevertheless, when the Japanese expedition failed to materialize, Lansing was as relieved as other American officials.

The hectic weeks of June and July, 1918, marked the high point of Lansing's effort to foster co-operation with Japan. During this time, the Wilson administration abandoned its opposition to the Siberian expedition and began to develop plans for

[10] *Lansing Papers,* II, 353-355.
[11] March 24, 1918, *Lansing Papers,* II, 357-358.

its operation. While Wilson seems to have approved the idea primarily to keep the Japanese straight, Lansing supported the scheme for quite different reasons. From the reports of a Red attack on Czechoslovakian troops which were moving eastward along the Trans-Siberian Railway, the shadow of a plan had begun to take shape late in May. An expedition to rescue the Czechs did not appear to Lansing to be as risky as one directed toward the occupation of Russian territory. The Siberian populace was less likely to be offended by the former than the latter. Moreover, there was much to recommend the mission. The United States had a moral obligation to assist a group which was fighting against the Germans and manifested a determination to carry on the fight. Nor was Lansing unmindful of benefits derived from complying in some measure with the requests of Britain and France. These powers would be placed under additional obligation to the United States at the peace conference. And finally, there was an important imponderable. Anti-Bolsheviks were reported to be flocking around the Czechs. The prospect of foreign aid might cause eastern Russians to join the fight in large numbers. If this proved the case, the United States might wish to consider support for these forces. Should the events not occur, the announced purpose of the expedition would permit a graceful withdrawal. At the outset Lansing was less concerned with the possibility of Japan's establishing a monopoly in Siberia than he was with obtaining from Japan troops and shipping which would promise the largest success for the venture.[12]

As soon as Wilson approved the expedition, Lansing went to work on plans. He laid a proposal before Ishii on July 8: the United States and Japan were each to send approximately seven thousand men to Vladivostok to guard the railway lines

[12] Lansing to Wilson, June 28, 1918, Wilson Papers, II, 141. "Memorandum on the Siberian Situation," July 4, 1918; "Memorandum of a Conference at the White House in Reference to the Siberian Situation," July 6, 1918, Lansing Collection, "Private Memoranda." Lansing to Allied Ambassador, July 17, 1918, *For. Rels., 1918, Russia,* II, 287-290.

along which the Czech forces were moving; Japan was to furnish arms and ammunition to the Czechs on the understanding that the United States was to share the expense and supplement Japanese supplies as rapidly as possible; American and Japanese forces were to control Vladivostok in conjunction with Czech forces already there; and a joint announcement indicating the intention to rescue the Czechs and pledging noninterference in Russia's affairs was to be issued by the two countries. Ishii agreed to refer these terms to his government and raised discussion of the purpose of the expedition. On the latter question the two men reached an understanding. Joint efforts were initially to be directed entirely toward helping the Czechs, but revision of aims might be discussed later. Concerning this prospect, Ishii commented:

> The possibilities of extending the program will depend very much upon the way the Siberian people view the present plan . . . and how other Russians will look upon it. This we cannot tell until our forces are actually landed at Vladivostok. That will test the question. If they are friendly, we can revise our program.

Lansing, who recorded the remarks, did not dissent.[13]

A conciliatory spirit pervaded subsequent discussions. The Japanese desired assurance that one of their officers would have command of the expedition. On Lansing's recommendation this was conceded by Wilson.[14] Japan balked at the limit placed on troop strength. The United States agreed to compromise, setting the number at ten thousand with the provision that Japan

[13] Lansing Memorandum, July 8, 1918, *For. Rels., 1918, Russia,* II, 267-268. House evidently understood Lansing's purpose in supporting the joint expedition. Commenting to Wilson on the conversation between Lansing and Ishii, House urged that the expedition not be converted into an anti-Japanese move. He concluded, "It has been my opinion for a long time that unless Japan was treated with more consideration regarding the right of her citizens to expand in nearby Asiatic undeveloped countries she would have to be reckoned with—and rightly so."—July 6, 1918, Wilson Papers, II, 144.

[14] Lansing to Wilson, July 10, 1918, *Lansing Papers,* II, 373. Note by Polk, July 16, 1918, Polk Papers, Polk Diary. For Lansing's reasoning on this concession see his comments on the expediency of giving Japan command. "Memorandum on German Domination in Siberia and Possible Means of Overcoming It," March 22, 1918, Lansing Collection, "Private Memoranda."

could discuss with the United States the dispatch of additional units.[15] Privately, Lansing was certain that Japan would shortly exceed the ten-thousand limit. He had insisted on a size for the first Japanese contingent which would not be much greater than that being sent by the United States only because he wished to avoid giving the Siberian populace the impression that Japan was seeking selfish advantage.[16] On one matter only did the Secretary take an inflexible position. Japan's draft of the public announcement concerning the purpose of the expedition contained reference to "special interests." The United States was successful in insisting that this be removed. Wilson and Lansing were agreed that the step was necessary in the event the United States wished to restrain Japanese actions in the future. Lansing was also concerned about the effect the reference might have on Russian sensibilities.[17]

While the war lasted, Lansing continued the co-operative policy even though the Japanese were increasingly inclined to act independently of the United States. On August 13 Japanese troops were reported to be heading toward the Manchurian border. Their professed objective was the protection of Manchuria from invasion by the Reds, an action which Japan maintained was provided for under an agreement made with China in May, 1918. The direction of the troop movements, however, indicated that the real purpose was to control the Chinese Eastern Railway. The inauguration of the move was a clear violation of the pledge made by Japan on August 3, in which Japan agreed to consult with the United States before sending troops to any point other than Vladivostok.[18] Other violations of Jap-

[15] Polk Memorandum, Aug. 3, 1918, Polk Papers, Polk Diary.

[16] Lansing to Polk, Aug. 3, 1918, Lansing Collection.

[17] Lansing rejected a French and British suggestion that they participate in the Siberian expedition. He feared such participation would give rise to the thought that efforts were being made to establish a pro-allied government in Russia. Lansing believed the success of the expedition depended on avoiding the spread of any such ideas. Lansing to Polk, Aug. 3, 1918, Lansing Collection.

[18] Morris to Lansing, Aug. 13, 1918, *For. Rels., 1918, Russia,* II, 343-344. Polk Memorandum, Aug. 3, 1918, Polk Papers, Polk Diary.

anese pledges were also noted. Japanese troop strength was developed far in excess of the agreed limit without consultation.[19] Japanese forces openly supported local militarists, ignoring the pledge to avoid interference in Russia's domestic affairs.[20] In a word, Japan seemed determined to cut loose from the United States. Lansing was disturbed by the knowledge, but he was unwilling to remonstrate with Japan. Between the launching of the expedition and the end of October, 1918, the State Department expressed to Tokyo nothing more than mild disapproval.[21] During the same period Lansing urged Wilson to order American troops to co-operate with the Japanese move into northern Manchuria.[22]

Lansing's policy was shaped partly by the continuing European war. Although peace feelers came out of Berlin in the autumn of 1918, the Wilson administration was by no means certain that the Central Powers were beaten. The feeling prevailed that nothing should interfere with the delivery of the knockout. For this reason Lansing was reluctant to start any trouble in Siberia. His policy was also influenced by his developing conviction that the joint expedition could indeed be used against the Bolsheviks. The Siberian population had exhibited no resentment toward the foreign troops. The Czechs and White Russians were reported to be fighting well. These events gave Japan's actions a bright aspect. By moving quickly the Japanese

[19] Lansing to Wilson, Aug. 18, 1918, *Lansing Papers,* II, 374-375.

[20] Morris to Lansing, Oct. 25, 1918, *For. Rels., 1918, Russia,* III, 278-280.

[21] In July a Japanese-inspired move to establish a Siberian government under the direction of the Russian Director of the Chinese Eastern Railway was reported to the State Department. The department asked Japan to disavow the report. MacMurray to Lansing, July 12; Polk to Morris, July 19, 1918, *For. Rels., 1918, Russia,* II, 278-279; 297-298. Two months later the State Department began to urge the placing of the Siberian railways under the control of an inter-Allied Commission. This effort was to create serious friction. Little pressure was applied, however, until the war ended. For correspondence in September and October, 1918, see *For. Rels., 1918, Russia,* III, 242-280.

[22] Long to Lansing, Aug. 17; Lansing to Wilson, Aug. 18, 1918, SD 861.00/2602 1/2.

could probably gain control of the Chinese Eastern Railway and thus open a supply line to anti-Bolshevik forces and create hope for the establishment of a center for resisting the spread of the revolution.[23] These prospects suggested the expediency of allowing the Japanese, at least for the moment, to take the lead. While Wilson failed to commit himself to the idea of an anti-Bolshevik crusade, he concurred with Lansing to the extent of agreeing that Czech forces should not be brought out of Siberia immediately and that the United States should not interfere with Japan's attempts to clear the railways of Bolsheviks.[24]

The end of World War I on November 11, 1918, terminated a phase of America's Far Eastern diplomacy which began with the Lansing-Ishii talks and embraced the first steps in the Siberian intervention. During this phase Lansing regarded the prosecution of the war and encouragement of anti-Bolshevik forces as primary American interests. The safeguarding of China's integrity, he felt, was at best a secondary concern. This arrangement of policy objectives brought Lansing once again into conflict with Wilson, who continued to emphasize the protection of China. The practical result of the conflict was the development of different understandings of the purpose of the Siberian expedition. Wilson's inclination to use American forces to oppose the Japanese was constantly checked by Lansing. The Secretary assumed that American-Japanese co-operation was vital to the prosecution of the war and campaign against the Bolsheviks. If the price of such co-operation were concessions to Japan's imperial aspirations, he was prepared to pay it. This explains Lansing's constant concern for Japanese sensibilities during the period just reviewed.

[23] The evolution of Lansing's thinking is suggested in the following document: "Memorandum on Intervention in Russia," June 12, 1918, Lansing Collection, "Private Memoranda." Lansing Memorandum, Aug. 20, 1918, *For. Rels., 1918, Russia,* II, 351. Lansing to Wilson, Sept. 9, 24, 1918, *Lansing Papers,* II, 381-384, 386-387.

[24] Lansing Memorandum, Aug. 20; Lansing to Morris, Aug. 30, 1918, *For. Rels., 1918, Russia,* II, 351, 239-241.

Lansing, however, was not prepared to grant Japan a free hand in East Asia. The spread of Japanese monopoly continued to concern him, but the problem was to devise ways of meeting the threat. While the war lasted, American resources for holding Japan in check were slim indeed. With the coming of peace another situation seemed likely to prevail. In 1914 Lansing had predicted that the end of fighting would release new American energies in the Orient and that these energies could be used advantageously in controlling Japanese expansion. The shooting had scarcely stopped in Europe when the Secretary began to test his theory.

11. Return To 1909

On November 16, 1918, Lansing announced to Ambassador Ishii a new American policy on Siberia. The Secretary, referring to the large number of Japanese troops there, said that Japan had broken her pledge to consult with the United States before dispatching more than the agreed number of men and had failed to use her forces in a co-operative manner. In seizing the Chinese Eastern Railway Japanese troops were establishing a monopoly which, Lansing held, "will arouse suspicions and prove open to exploitation. Such a monopoly is certainly opposed to the purpose of this Government to assist Russia but [*sic*] also its views regarding China." Lansing asked Japan to demonstrate that she was not using the Siberian intervention to advance her imperial designs by agreeing to the establishment of an inter-allied railway commission. This commission, which was to be headed by the American engineer, John P. Stevens, would operate the Siberian and Chinese Eastern systems on behalf of the Russians and not for the advantage of any foreign power.[1]

This plain talk contrasted sharply with the studied ambiguity of the Lansing-Ishii conversations. In effect the United States gave notice of her intention to scrutinize Japan's activity in China and Siberia with the purpose of opposing any efforts to win "special privilege." The significance of this sudden decision

[1] Lansing to Morris, *For. Rels., 1918, Russia,* II, 433-435.

to check Japan's advance derived only partly from the fact that it marked the resumption of the American-Japanese rivalry. The decision was also important because it reflected the beginning of a new attempt by Lansing to effect a settlement in East Asia. This attempt, like the one which preceded it, focused on the resolution of American-Japanese differences, but the tactics employed to achieve the settlement were decidedly altered. Wilson's refusal to approve a bargain with Japan and the growing influence of expansionists within the Japanese government caused Lansing to devise new plans. From November, 1918, until the summer of the following year, Lansing urged that the United States stand firmly against Japanese expansion. Such a stance, he believed, would convince the Japanese government of the futility of continuing a rivalry with the United States.

The inauguration of a firm policy was occasioned by the fear that the Japanese military was destroying hope for the development of an anti-Bolshevik center in Siberia. In dealing with Russians, Japanese officers had concentrated entirely on militarists such as Dimitri Horvath and Grigori Semenov or groups led by Cossack adventurers. The Japanese aim was apparently the establishment of a regime opposed to the Reds. Lansing did not object to this purpose, but he was confident that the effort had no hope of success. The Russian militarists and Cossacks were reported to be adventurers of the worst kind. The regimes set up by them had no firm base of popular support. According to Ambassador Morris, who had been sent to Siberia to make a firsthand survey, it would be a mistake for the powers to align themselves with any of the existing Siberian regimes. Rather, the United States and Japan should concentrate on putting the railways into full operation. This would permit the supplying of the forces fighting the Bolsheviks and the populace behind the battle lines. The aid would not only contribute to the defeat of the Red armies, but it would also foster the development of a genuinely representative government. This latter idea was based on the assumption that if local governments succeeded in resolving pressing economic problems, they would coalesce to form an anti-Bolshevik regime.[2] Lansing, convinced that the Japanese protégés were incapable of creating a stable government, decided to pursue the plan suggested by Morris.[3]

The Secretary's first step was to seek Wilson's approval. He began in late August by urging the President to appoint a commission which would direct the rehabilitation of Siberia.[4] This was followed by an attempt to have Wilson broaden the stated purposes of the American expedition. Red atrocities were cited to justify such revision. The United States should announce its determination to aid Siberians in establishing a government which would be independent of the "blood thirsty" Bolsheviks.[5] Americans, Lansing argued, would approve the move if they were informed of its necessity. To alert the public, he suggested that he deliver a speech in which he would dwell on the need to continue the war until the spirit of "Prussianism" was everywhere eliminated. Used in this context, "Prussiansm" was manifest in the determination of the Russian revolutionaries to establish a dictatorship of the proletariat.[6] This latter proposal was too much for Wilson. The President, unwilling to commit the country to a new crusade in the closing weeks of the war, refused to approve the speech.[7] Yet he did go part of the way with Lansing. On September 18, 1918, he designated a com-

[2] Lansing to Morris, Sept. 4; Morris to Lansing, Sept. 23; Oct. 18, 1918, *For. Rels., 1918, Russia,* II, 366, 387-390, 414-415.

[3] Lansing to Wilson, Sept. 24, 1918, *Lansing Papers,* II, 386-387. Lansing to Morris, Oct. 23, 1918, *For. Rels., 1918, Russia,* II, 416.

[4] For evidence of Lansing's early interest in an economic program, see his "Memorandum on Intervention in Russia," June 12, 1918, Lansing Collection, "Private Memoranda." A progress report was given in Gordon Auchincloss to House, Aug. 21, 1918, House Papers.

[5] Lansing to Wilson, Aug. 22, 1918; Lansing to Wilson (enclosing George Kennan to Lansing, Aug. 9, 1918), Aug. 14, 1918, Wilson Papers, II, 146, 147. Lansing to Wilson, Aug. 29; Sept. 9, 1918, *Lansing Papers,* II, 379, 381-384.

[6] Lansing to Wilson (enclosing draft of speech), Sept. 23, 1918, Wilson Papers, II, 149.

[7] The reasons appear in House to Wilson, Sept. 25, 1918, Wilson Papers, II, 149.

mittee of high ranking officials to take charge of the shipping and distributing of supplies to Siberia. Six days later he departed from the prepared text of a speech at the Metropolitan Opera House in New York to declare his intention to "stand by the Russians." The Secretary, it appears, was making headway in his representations to the White House.

The attempt to enlist Japan's support of the developing program was postponed until the end of the war. The delay was due to peculiar problems presented by Japanese politics. Since August, 1918, Japan's Siberian policy had been controlled by the military. Japanese troop movements had been undertaken without consultation with civilian authorities. The function of Japanese diplomats had seemed simply to explain as well as they could what the army had done. It did not appear that the United States could suggest a change in Japanese policy without offending the delicate sensibilities of the military.[8] Such an offense, it was noted earlier, seemed likely to result in Japan's dropping out of or changing sides in the war. Thus it was not merely a coincidence that Lansing withheld an announcement of the new American policy on Siberia until a week after the Armistice had been signed. To Lansing's mind the defeat of the Central Powers outweighed any other American objective.

By the time the shift in American policy was announced, Lansing had developed an intricate plan for bringing the United States and Japan to an agreement. The key to its accomplishment was the transfer of decision-making authority within the Japanese government into the hands of moderates. In January, 1917, Lansing had told Wilson concerning Japanese extremists, "I am disposed to believe that the more we yield to Japan the more we shall be asked to yield and that a firm stand upon our undoubted rights will compel a modification of Japanese demands. . . .[9]" These remarks were made in reference to pressures which were being exerted on Peking, but recent experience

[8] Morris to Lansing, July 13; Sept. 8, 1918, *For. Rels., 1918, Russia,* III, 245-246.

[9] Lansing to Wilson, Jan. 17, 1917, SD 893.51/1746a.

indicated that they also applied to Siberia. The failure of the United States to protest Japanese moves there had apparently been interpreted in military circles as indications of American weakness, an interpretation which in turn gave rise to the idea that American wishes could safely be ignored. As long as the militarists retained the initiative, Lansing doubted that agreement could be reached on any issue. At the same time, the apparent eagerness of the Japanese Foreign Ministry to cooperate with the United States during the months when the Siberian expedition was under discussion suggested that there remained in Japan officials who wished to avoid the resumption of a dangerous rivalry. If the United States frustrated the aims of the Japanese military, the action would perhaps assist these moderates in gaining control of foreign policy.[10]

America's circumstances at the end of the war were such as to make feasible a policy of firmness. The end of hostilities provided new resources for dealing with Japan. The prospect of a Japanese-German alliance was no longer a frightening spectre which imposed restraint on American diplomats.[11] American investors were supplied with vast new capital resources which might be converted to political purposes. And finally, the war itself had provided a practical demonstration of America's ability to organize a tremendous armed force and to use that force effectively thousands of miles from its home base. There can be no doubt that Lansing recognized these advantages and planned to make use of them.[12] Earlier in 1918 he recorded confidently in his record of daily appointments, "[Assistant Secretary] Long

[10] A statement of the assumption is contained in Polk to the American Commission to Negotiate the Peace (hereinafter cited as Am. Com.), Dec. 21, 1918, *For. Rels., 1919, The Paris Peace Conference* (Washington, 1942-1947), II, 517-518. These volumes hereinafter cited as *For. Rels., 1919, P. P. C.* For evidence of Lansing's awareness of this assumption prior to December see the entry concerning Vance McCormick in the Secretary's Desk Diary, Nov. 9, 1918, Lansing Collection.

[11] Stanley K. Hornbeck to Lansing, July 11, 1919, Lansing Collection, summarizes the evidence on German-Japanese contacts.

[12] Lansing, *War Memoirs,* p. 285.

on the Far East and Japanese control in China. Pointed out to him increased prestige of U. S. if we win [the war]."[13]

Lansing had still another reason for thinking that Japanese moderates could gain control of foreign policy. On September 29, 1918, Count Terauchi, faced by growing domestic unrest, resigned from the Premiership. He was succeeded by Takashi Hara, the "Great Commoner." This change was significant in that it challenged the leadership of the established oligarchy. Since the Restoration, the Satsuma and Choshu clans had perpetuated arrangements which had given the military a pre-eminent position in government. Hara's accession to the Premiership broke tradition. As the first untitled man to hold office, his claim to leadership stemmed from the support given him by the Seiyukai party. Thus Japan was led by a party politician, a man who was indebted partly for his prominence to commercial, industrial, and financial elements, and who might be expected to be more responsive to these groups than were his predecessors. As to the attitude of these business groups, the State Department already had some information. Charles Denby, who had been assigned to survey American prospects in the Far East, and Ambassador Morris reported in the spring of 1918 that the Japanese business community viewed its own development as being tied to the expansion of trade with the United States.[14] These reports confirmed Ambasador Guthrie's thesis concerning the desire of Japanese businessmen to have their country settle its differences with the United States. Further evidence on the Hara Ministry's attitude was contained in statements originating from high Japanese sources. On October 2, 1918, the *New York Times* quoted Dr. J. Ingram Bryan, who wrote in the *Japan Magazine,* as saying that the Seiyukai would work closely with the United States in Siberian affairs. A few days later Hara announced that a primary task of his Ministry was

[13] May 21, 1918.

[14] Denby to Polk, May 8, 1918, Polk Papers, "Far East: Minor Papers, 1918." Morris to Lansing, March 7, 1918, SD 793.94/673.

the clearing away of difficulties with the United States.[15] Against the background just sketched these statements appeared to be something more than the usual polite talk. They were perhaps hints that important Japanese officials continued to regard a settlement with the United States as an important objective.

Evidence that Hara's professions had substance was shortly forthcoming. Following Lansing's talk with Ishii on November 16, Ambassador Morris continued American representations in Tokyo. In December the Foreign Office admitted that the sending of large numbers of troops to Siberia was a mistake. Nearly 14,000 troops were to be withdrawn immediately, and 34,000 more were to be brought out in the near future.[16] These steps would cut Japanese troop strength by more than half. The announcement of troop reduction was followed by an offer to negotiate on the establishment of the inter-allied railway board. A month later (January, 1919) the negotiations resulted in an agreement to set up a control board, an organization incorporating most of the features desired by Americans.[17] The Hara Ministry had conceded almost everything asked of it.

For Lansing these events had two aspects: the immediate importance of the Japanese concessions sprang from the renewed hope they gave for success of an anti-Bolshevik crusade. The appearance of the Kolchak regime in November, 1918, provided new evidence of resistance to the Reds within eastern Russia. If Japan followed her concessions with other co-operative measures, the Siberian populace might yet receive the aid it needed to establish an independent regime. A second, but no less important, aspect was the indication that a formula had been discovered for the solution of the broad range of American-

[15] *New York Times,* Oct. 21, 1918. Newsmen reported the impression that the new Ministry would be less subject to military pressures than its predecessor.

[16] Polk Memorandum of a conversation with the Japanese Ambassador, n. d., Polk Papers, "Far East: Japanese Embassy, 1918." Morris to Lansing, Dec. 27, 1918, *For. Rels., 1918, Russia,* III, 301-303.

[17] Lansing to Polk, Jan. 21, 1919, *For. Rels., 1919,* (Washington, 1937), pp. 243-244.

Japanese problems. In his conversation with Ishii on November 16, Lansing was acting on a hypothesis. He was not certain that the Hara Ministry would react to a firm policy the way he hoped. Nor was he certain that Japanese moderates had enough political strength to assert authority over the military. The fact that events worked out according to the Secretary's conjecture taught a lesson concerning future dealings with Japan. This lesson's meaning was spelled out by Acting Secretary Polk in a cable to the American Peace Delegation: while the Hara Ministry's concessions represented a victory over extremists, the American government should not assume that the authority of Japanese moderates was established. The Japanese General Staff continued to control Siberian affairs, and the Staff was supported by public opinion which tended to endorse a strong policy on all Asiatic questions. The Hara Ministry was sincerely convinced that Japan's best interests would be served by cordial co-operation with the United States, but without popular support the Ministry was too weak to force a showdown with the military. If the United States were to obtain Japanese co-operation, a way must be found to place the policy of firmness on a continuing basis. Perhaps a complete understanding between the United States and European powers having an interest in the Far East would strengthen the hand of liberal groups against the ambitious programs of the military.[18]

A few weeks earlier Polk's suggestion would have seemed doctrinaire. While Britain and France had been worried by Japanese expansion, the war had prevented them from raising any opposition. As the fighting drew to a close, however, the State Department received intimations of a willingness on the part of those two countries to join forces with the United States. The agency through which the powers proposed to co-operate was a revived and reorganized banking consortium.

Lansing's interest in reviving a consortium, it will be recalled, extended to the unsuccessful effort to have the old Amer-

[18] Polk to Am. Com., Dec. 21, 1918, *For. Rels., 1919, P. P. C.*, II, 517-518.

ican Group make a loan to China in the summer of 1916. Although the collapse of this effort was discouraging, Lansing, faced with an increasing number of Japanese loans to Peking, became increasingly convinced that the consortium should be reactivated and America should play a major role in the organization. As a form of international control on loans to China, a consortium would stop Japan's practice of obtaining valuable concessions in return for cash advances on loans negotiated with Peking war lords. Moreover, revival of the consortium idea, insofar as it conveyed the impression of vigorous action, would demonstrate the American intention of taking effective steps to support its Far Eastern policy. In January, 1917, Lansing wrote a long letter to Wilson recommending obliquely consideration of renewed government support for bankers who were willing to activate the old American Group.[19] Later in the year his advice became quite direct. After hearing that European members of the Six Power Consortium were interested in doing business with China and that key members of the American Group were also interested, Lansing wrote, "My own view is that the whole question, being of so much importance to our future relations in the Far East, ought to be considered with little regard to the past."[20] In taking this position Lansing moved in advance of his State Department colleagues. Presumably he wished to use the consortium idea for additional bargaining power in his upcoming talks with Ishii. Before the end of the summer, however, the acceleration of Japanese financial operations in China prompted Long, Reinsch, and Williams to support his view.[21]

Wilson was not immediately persuaded by the advice. Following the failure of the effort to reactivate the Six Power Consortium, the President reverted to the idea that an international

[19] SD 893.51/1746a.

[20] To Wilson, June 25, 1917, SD 893.51/1799a.

[21] Williams Memorandum, June 26, 1917, Long Papers, "The Chinese Loans, 1918." Long to Polk, July 12, 1917, Polk Papers. Reinsch to Lansing, Aug. 6, 1917, *For. Rels., 1917,* pp. 135-136.

monopoly over loans provided a means for coercing China and that independent American loans remained China's best hope. The impracticality of the idea had to be demonstrated once more before Wilson would change his mind. This was done in the early autumn of 1917.

The Peking government then approached Japan for a £10,000,000 loan for currency reform and administrative purposes. Technically the money was to come from the Six Power Consortium, but since the Japanese Group was the only one in a position to advance funds, the loan would in reality come from Japan. The conditions of the loan were expected to be such as to enable Japan to claim substantial "special privilege" in China Proper. This latter prospect caused alarm in London. The British urged Peking to cancel her application, but the war lords, who were anxious to obtain funds to bolster themselves against forces raised in south China, were not to be dissuaded. When China's determination became evident, the British turned to the United States. Wilson was asked to approve the re-entry of American bankers into the Six Power Consortium. In this way control would be imposed upon Japanese activities.[22]

Wilson, alert to the threat to China's independence but convinced that much harm would be done through a revival of the Six Power Group, directed the State Department to plan a large American loan which was to be made under a law providing for financial aid to America's allies.[23] These funds were to provide China with an alternative to the Japanese loan. In consequence, Wilson was deeply disappointed to learn a few days after he had given his instruction that Peking seemed ready to take America's money and Japan's as well.[24] Only when this was clear was the President willing to change his mind. Lansing recalled later that early in November, 1917, American partic-

[22] Colville Barclay to Lansing, Aug. 21; Reinsch to Lansing, Sept. 7; British Embassy to Lansing, Oct. 3, 1917, *For. Rels., 1917,* pp. 136-137; 144-145.

[23] Lansing to Reinsch, Sept. 20, 1917, *For. Rels., 1917,* p. 142.

[24] Reinsch to Lansing, Sept. 28; British Embassy to Lansing, Oct. 3, 1917, *For. Rels., 1917,* pp. 144-146.

ipation in a consortium was recommended to the President "in no uncertain terms, by me, and was, by him, approved in principle."[25] By the time the decision was reached, however, another obstacle had appeared. The Treasury Department was preparing for a Liberty Loan drive and urged that nothing be done to compete with its call for funds. Since financing the war had first priority, planning for a multi-power loan to China was delayed until June, 1918.[26]

When the consortium idea was brought up again, the plans of 1917 were altered. Initially the State Department had conceived of supporting the participation of an American Group in the existing Six Power Consortium. This organization had been established to make administrative loans to the Chinese government. Loans for other purposes, such as, for example, industrial loans, were outside its preserve. The new State Department plans called for the forming of an organization with a broader scope of operations, one which would make all types of loans to China. The ultimate purpose was to avoid difficulties from arising over the classification of a loan. As long as the Six Power Consortium continued, State Department officials were confident that Japan would continue to make independent grants to China under the pretense of their being industrial loans. The new plan would tie Japan's hands.[27]

The idea of expanding consortium operations originated with British and American firms having an interest in railway construction. Sometime early in 1918 British and French companies which controlled options for construction of the line connecting Canton and Hankow (the so-called Hukuang system), opened negotiations with the Siems-Carey Construction

[25] Lansing to William C. Redfield, Jan. 18, 1918, SD 793.94/662. Lansing to Reinsch, Nov. 9, 1917, *For. Rels., 1917,* p. 153.

[26] Long Memoranda, January 22; June 20, 1918, Long Papers, "The Chinese Loans, 1918"; "China, June 1, 1918-December 31, 1918." Lansing to Wilson, June 20, 1918, *For. Rels., 1918* (Washington, 1930), pp. 169-171.

[27] The urgent need for applying effective control over Japanese loans was recognized in the department. Reinsch to Lansing, February 12; April 30, 1918, *For. Rels., 1918,* pp. 84-93. Williams to Lansing, Long Papers, "Memoranda, China, 1919." Morris to Lansing, April 19, 1918, SD 793.94/683.

Company and American International Corporation. The American banking firm was asked to supply capital for three hundred miles of road, a sum which would complete the line. If this were done, Siems-Carey would be admitted to the project and given certain other concessions. Among the latter were guarantees of contracts for equipping the newly completed road and certain connecting lines. In making the proposition British management appears to have given assurances that it would urge its government to abandon its claim to a sphere of influence. The French government indicated that it might go along with the scheme. The American firms were definitely interested, but they lacked capital. They appealed to the State Department for assistance. Out of this appeal came the plans for a new consortium.[28]

The State Department was to be disappointed in its hopes for the quick establishment of a new banker's organization. No trouble was experienced in obtaining Wilson's fresh approval of the idea. The President reaffirmed his assent on June 21.[29] Nor was there any difficulty in working out details for the organization of the American bankers. Assistant Secretary Long, working under Lansing's close supervision, developed plans for broadening the membership in the old Group and pooling options on various projects. The State Department and bankers were fully agreed by the middle of July.[30] The responsibility for the delay was Great Britain's. The British objected to the idea of broadening consortium operations to include industrial projects. Great Britain, the United States was reminded, had dropped industrial loans from the projected operations of the Six Power Group at Japan's insistence. Since the Japanese had

[28] Draft of letter, Lansing to Wilson. Marked "not sent." Feb. 11, 1918; Long Memorandum, Feb. 14, 1918, Long Papers, "Memoranda, China, 1917-1918." Walter H. Page to Lansing, April 9, 1918; Lansing to Wilson, June 20, 1918, *For. Rels., 1918,* pp. 145-146; 169-171.

[29] Wilson to Lansing, *For. Rels., 1918,* p. 171.

[30] Long Memorandum, June 26, 1918; Long to Lansing, July 2, 1918, Long Papers, "Memoranda, China, 1918." Certain American Bankers to Lansing; Lansing to Certain American Bankers, July 8, 9, 1918, *For. Rels., 1918,* pp. 172-175.

not changed their minds, it seemed inexpedient to raise the question while the war continued. Consortium negotiations were thus at a standstill when the Armistice was signed.[31]

While the State Department would have preferred an immediate agreement, it was not gloomy over the British delaying tactics. The British attitude was presumed to be dictated by the necessity of placating an ally.[32] When the fighting stopped, London could undoubtedly be persuaded to accept the American view. There was clear evidence that Britain was planning on American assistance in resisting Japanese expansion in China. Her expressed willingness to allow American capital to enter the British sphere of influence and her desire to have the United States take the lead in reviving international financing in China have already been noted. To this list may be added the British request, which was made in November, 1917, that the United States inquire about Japan's intentions of asking China to accept the postponed provisions of Group V of the Twenty-one Demands. While the inquiry was not made, Britain's purpose was clear. She was depending on the United States to block a widely rumored move which, if it were actually made, would seriously injure British interests.[33] Furthermore, the State Department expected that British policy would be influenced by representations of powerful financial interests.[34] Certain British firms, it has been noted, had already made clear their desire to co-operate in China with American bankers and contractors. Additional pressure would be exerted by American financiers. Late in 1918 J. P. Morgan, who was a key figure in plans to establish a new consortium, divulged to the State Department his plan to travel to Britain and France early the following year. He was prepared to urge strongly that his foreign colleagues support the American consortium plan. Since Morgan was by

[31] R. S. Miller Memorandum, Nov. 29, 1918, Long Papers, "Memoranda, Japan, 1917-1918."

[32] Polk to MacMurray, August 10, 1918, *For. Rels., 1918,* p. 188.

[33] Long Memorandum, Nov. 3, 1917, Long Papers, "Memoranda, China, 1917-1918."

[34] W. H. Page to Lansing, Jan. 1, 1918, *For. Rels., 1918,* pp. 137-138.

then an international financial leader, it did not seem too much to presume his advice would receive a hearing.[35] Thus, the State Department did not think Britain's assent would be delayed long after the war ended. When this was obtained, France and Japan would fall into line. France would acquiesce easily; Japan would be more difficult, but she would experience difficulty in electing another course. If she remained outside, Japanese bankers would be isolated from Western financial centers, an eventuality which they were determined to avoid. With the Hara Ministry in office the desires of the business community would carry great weight.[36]

By the end of 1918 Wilson's Far Eastern policy had gone around the circle. Upon taking office the President had abandoned the tactics of the Taft administration, which had sought to control Japan by enlisting the co-operation of other powers. Wilson intended to safeguard China's integrity through independent action. Six and a half years later he admitted the futility of this line and approved a return to procedures which had been adopted in 1909. The new American policy was evident in plans to establish an inter-allied board to manage Russian railways and to encourage American bankers to participate in a reorganized consortium.

During the interim between the signing of the Armistice and opening of the Peace Conference, an optimistic glow seemed to settle over the State Department's outlook on Far Eastern affairs. Japan's announcement that she would withdraw most of her troops from Siberia and enter serious discussion of the operation of the Russian railways combined with Britain's apparent willingness to co-operate with the United States to give the new American policy every prospect for success. As Lansing sailed

[35] Long Memorandum, Dec. 30, 1918, Long Papers, "The Chinese Loan, 1918."

[36] In recommending the consortium idea to Wilson, Lansing remarked, "It will be pleasing no doubt to China and Japan." June 20, 1918, *For. Rels., 1918*, pp. 145-146. For further evidence of Japan's awareness of America's financial strength, see Ambassador Ishii's remarks at the beginning of the last Liberty Loan drive. *New York Times*, Oct. 10, 1918.

from New York harbor aboard the *George Washington* with the American Peace Delegation, he released some carrier pigeons which he had brought from Watertown. The birds carried to Lansing's relatives expressions of the Secretary's deep hope that the peace negotiations would effect a lasting international settlement. Clearly, Lansing's thinking, as had been the case throughout the war, was focused primarily on Europe, but it is also evident that his thought was not confined to Europe alone. The Secretary was planning to use the Paris Peace Conference to put the finishing touches on his scheme to bring Japan into line with American policy. If these plans materialized, there was indeed reason to hope for peace in the Far East.

12. "A Veritable Millstone About Our Necks"

Lansing looked thin and tired upon his arrival in Paris in December, 1918. Since entering the State Department, he had maintained a grueling schedule. He had entered his office precisely at nine o'clock each morning and had gone home at six. On most evenings he had attended official functions or had worked at home. His weekends had seldom been free from official business. During much of the time, his health had not been good. He had sugar diabetes, and the insulin treatment, which was then new therapy, had caused trouble. Frequently he had abstained from eating for a day in order to adjust himself to the medication. The result of these things went deeper than a change in appearance. His memory was not as sharp as formerly, and his temper flared from beneath his placid exterior more quickly than was customary. These symptoms of weariness, however, did not indicate diminished determination to carry through his programs. Early in the peace negotiations he remarked that it was "time for us to have it out once and for all with Japan."[1] That this was not an idle observation was soon demonstrated by his effort to prevent Japan's establishing a title to Germany's rights and privileges in Shantung.

The battle Lansing prepared to wage was not destined to be an easy one. Japan went to Paris demanding the unconditional

[1] Minutes of the Meeting of the Am. Com., Feb. 6, 1919, *For. Rels., 1919, P. P. C.,* XI, 21.

cession of German interests in Shantung as part of her share of the war spoils, a claim for which she could muster strong support. Japanese troops occupied portions of the province, especially the vital Tsingtao-Tsinan Railway. Japan had obtained from China treaty provisions supporting her contentions. As a result of the settlement of May 25, 1915, Japan gained free disposal of German rights. This concession was affirmed in a subsequent treaty concluded between Japan and China on September 24, 1918. Indeed, this latter document went beyond the 1915 agreement. According to its terms, China agreed to Japan's policing the Shantung railway and engaging in certain other practices which were intended to safeguard Japanese interests. Furthermore, Japan had negotiated secret treaties with her European allies in which the latter agreed to support Japan's claims in Shantung and to Germany's island colonies lying north of the equator. Finally, this complex of treaties had the backing of Japanese opinion. As has been noted, the war intensified Japanese nationalism. Increasingly, elements within Japan (this was especially true of the military) had come to regard East Asia as an exclusive area of operations for their country. To these nationalists, fulfilment of Japan's desire in Shantung held a significance extending far beyond the economic and strategic importance of the province: Shantung was a symbol of Japan's prestige and power. The very importance of the groups adhering to the view meant that the Hara Ministry was under heavy pressure to make as much as possible out of Japan's bargaining position.

Lansing was certainly aware of all of these things. He had followed closely Japan's moves to entrench herself in Shantung. Most of the cables concerning Japanese activities there crossed his desk. He was fully apprised of the terms of the Sino-Japanese treaties. Most historians now believe that he and Wilson knew far more about the secret treaties of 1917 than they were willing to admit to the Senate Foreign Relations Committee. A reworking of the evidence reveals no reason to doubt this assumption. And finally, the record of Japanese behavior in Siberia was indicative of extremist ambitions. Thus it is evident that Lansing realized a hard fight was ahead if the United States sought to deny Japanese claims. It was a battle, however, which Lansing believed must be fought and won. The admission of Japanese claims would seriously damage a broad range of American interests in East Asia.

For one thing, Japan's demand that the powers recognize her claims to a sphere of influence in Shantung threatened American commercial opportunities in China. American contracts for railway construction and flood control would be jeopardized. As has been noted, the execution of these contracts depended upon the powers' admitting American capital to their spheres of influence. If the United States failed to contest Japan's attempt to extend her monopoly, European states would be provided with a basis for opposing the Americans' entry into their spheres. Beyond this lay the danger that a Japanese victory would result in the development of Chinese enmity toward the United States. While the Paris Conference was in progress, Reinsch cabled an illuminating description of official Chinese thinking about America's record in China:

> As against this popular enthusiasm for things American, there is a strongly marked view of cynicism in the higher official view of the United States. She is credited with being sincere in her professions of friendship for China, but it is believed that her actions fall short of her words. That in practice she does not consider China of sufficient importance to justify a forcible insistence on the *bona-fide* application of the "open door" principle. Similarly with regard to the economic development of China, it is difficult to convince these officials that the United States is serious in the proposals which she has made from time to time for railway and other construction work. They point to the number of past failures to carry out widely advertised plans and to the delay in commencing work on more recent concessions, and conclude again that more has been promised than will be performed. For these reasons it is of great importance that every effort should be made to give some tangible proof of the sincerity of American enterprise in China.[2]

[2] March 10, 1919, *For. Rels., 1919,* I, 282.

This advice, which was merely a summation of ideas embodied in many of the Minister's earlier cables, must be measured against the background of Chinese expectations. China went to Paris thinking that the United States would stand firmly for the abolition of "special privilege" in Shantung. Her delegates were encouraged to think this by America's own actions. Wilson's wartime pronouncements had stressed the importance of national self-determination and development. Moreover the State Department had sanctioned the inclusion in China's peace proposals of the item specifying the return of German rights and privileges.[3] Failure to meet the hope thus generated would probably have a disastrous effect on American prestige. Peking, which was oriented toward Japan anyway, was likely to interpret concessions to the Japanese view as conclusive evidence that the United States was not serious about China. In the face of that opinion Americans could not expect much success in obtaining a share of the projects which would develop as China developed into a modern state.[4]

A firm stand on Shantung was also important to Lansing because of its bearing on future Japanese policy. The Secretary viewed the defeat of Japanese pretensions in Shantung as a key part of the campaign to wrest the initiative in the forma-

[3] See notation of Lansing's conference with the Chinese Minister, Oct. 23, 1918, Lansing Collection, Desk Diary. Long Memoranda, November 6, 20, 1918, Long Papers. Reinsch to Lansing, Nov. 24, 1918, *For. Rels., 1919, P. P. C.,* II, 507-508.

[4] Lansing was as concerned with the future of American commerce in China during his last months in office as he had been earlier. In discussing a replacement for Reinsch, who resigned in 1919, Lansing recommended the new man have a fundamental idea of commerce and industry. Lansing to Wilson, August, 1919, Wilson Papers, II, 161. His thinking was also reflected in a memorandum drafted after he left the State Department. This read: "It is time that it [the State Department] looked at business from the point of view of the American businessman, seeking practical ways to help and volunteering such help whenever possible, rather than spending its time in formulating reasons why it should refuse assistance of any sort, and making those who appeal to the State Department feel that their chief difficulty is in persuading their own Government that they are honest and acting in good faith."—"Memorandum on the General Situation of American Foreign Policies," Feb. 16, 1922, Lansing Collection, "Private Memoranda."

tion of Japanese policy from the military. Japan's peace terms were reported to have been formulated jointly by the Foreign, Army, and Navy ministries. It was further understood, an understanding which subsequent research confirmed, that the Army and Navy took the lead in insisting on the retention of German privileges in Shantung.[5] To Lansing the implications of this report were clear: concessions on Shantung would encourage the Army and Navy to press for continued independent action.[6] Such a Japanese policy would complicate and, perhaps, render impossible the adjustment of important questions. Although Hara had pledged support of interallied management of the Russian railways, Japanese Army officers were dealing as before with local Russian militarists. Thus, as the Peace Conference went forward, independent Japanese action imperiled chances for the emergence of a stable Siberian regime. In another realm Lansing anticipated that the military Ministers would resist strongly the organization of a new consortium. Earlier there was no Japanese objection to the reactivation of the old Six Power organization. Japan could dominate that organization and, thus, could pursue an independent line. The organization being projected by the United States, however, would permit less freedom of action. For this reason Hara would come under strong pressure to resist American plans. When viewed in this context, the Shantung question assumed dimensions that have generally passed unnoticed. To the status of the province was tied the larger issue of American-Japanese co-operation. Lansing was convinced that defeat of Japan's pretensions would provide a crucial victory for Japanese moderates and would thus strengthen the prospects for co-operation. The opposite outcome would increase the prestige of the Japanese military and would

[5] Morris to Lansing, Nov. 13, 1918, *For. Rels., 1919, P. P. C.,* I, 489.

[6] There was no doubt as to how the Japanese military regarded evidence of weakness. On Nov. 16, 1918, Lansing inquired of Morris whether the withdrawal of American troops from Siberia would embarrass the Japanese and prompt the military to be more co-operative. Morris replied that the military would welcome the move. Nov. 16, 20, 1918, *For. Rels., 1918, Russia,* II, 433-436.

result in the intensification of the American-Japanese rivalry.

It is difficult to overemphasize Lansing's conviction on this latter point. World War I had caused him to develop decided views about governments which were dominated by military men. Germany, he believed, had evolved insatiable desires which she then attempted to realize through use of force. The idea that a German victory over Britain and France would pose great dangers for the United States led Lansing to press for American intervention in the war as early as 1915.[7] At Paris, Lansing, worn by years of exhausting work, influenced by emotions carried over from the war, and alarmed by the spectre of the Bolshevik revolution, was greatly exercised by the prospect of Japan's coming under the influence of militarists. Lansing agreed with Reinsch's observation that the policies of the Japanese military could only lead to "evil and destruction," and with Williams' observation that, "The spirit of Japan is that of Prussia, whom the Japanese leaders openly admire and whose government they chose for a model."[8] Before the peace negotiations ended the Secretary was referring to Japan as a "Prussianized state" whose policies were inimical to those of the United States.[9] The intensity of his belief accounted for his later bitterness over the Shantung decision. In his communications to Wilson and in his memoirs, Lansing, who was apparently hoping to enlist sympathetic support for return of German rights and privileges to China, emphasized the injustice to China of the

[7] Daniel M. Smith, "Robert Lansing and the Formulation of American Neutrality Policies, 1914-1915," *The Mississippi Valley Historical Review,* XLIII (June, 1956), 59-81.

[8] Reinsch to Wilson, Jan. 13, 1919, House Papers. Williams Comment, Jan. 16, 1919, SD PPC 185.1152/17.

[9] For example, see "The Japanese Claims to Kiau Chau and Shantung Admitted," May 1, 1919, Lansing Collection, "Private Memoranda." Lansing's judgment was not based on Reinsch's observations alone. On August 22, 1918, W. W. Willoughby, a Johns Hopkins University political scientist who was traveling in the Orient, reported that Japan's "aggressive international policy" was due in large measure to the distinctly Prussian cast of her constitutional and political philosophy. The report, which had been requested by Lansing, received considerable attention in the department. Willoughby to Long, Long Papers, "Memoranda, China, 1917-1918."

Japanese claims. This desire to do justice to China, however, was acquired too quickly to appear authentic. Lansing, unlike Wilson, subordinated China's welfare to concrete American objectives. To Lansing the profoundly disturbing thing about the Shantung decision was not the damage done to China itself but the new difficulties that it presented for the advance of American interests in East Asia.

While he anticipated a hard fight with Japan, he was confident that the United States could win. Shortly after negotiations started at Paris, the State Department cabled Peking, "China has a good chance to recover possession of German rights in Shantung."[10] Such a statement seemed to the department not to rest on wishful thinking but rather on hard facts. During a meeting of the American Peace Commissioners, Henry White, noting that the Japanese had undoubtedly been disturbed by the extent and energy of the American war effort, remarked that "of course, if it came to a direct issue between us, Japan would be in a greatly inferior position because of her relatively inferior economic and financial strength." Lansing, who had earlier reached the same conclusion, replied that "this was absolutely true," and that it was "America's duty to support China."[11] At the outset, then, whether America had the strength to deal effectively with Japan was not important to Lansing. What was unanswered was whether the United States would make full use of her bargaining power.

Lansing was cheered by initial developments. Japan suffered reverses during the first days of the Conference. On January 23 Lloyd George asked immediate consideration of "Oriental and Colonial questions." Japan moved into the opening by coupling her strictly colonial claims in the north Pacific with the more complicated claims in Shantung. Her strategy was simple: the powers would admit that German rights should accrue to Japan. Japan would then be free to negotiate independ-

[10] Polk to Reinsch, Jan. 31, 1919, SD 793.94/762.

[11] Minutes of the Meeting of the Am. Com., Feb. 6, 1919, *For. Rels., 1919, P. P. C.*, XI, 21.

ently with Peking on the ultimate disposition of the Shantung question. But the play was blocked by Wilson. On January 27 the President succeeded in isolating Shantung from Japan's colonial claims. The next day he confronted Japanese delegates with Chinese representatives who argued before the Council of Ten for direct cession of German rights to China. The move destroyed Japan's hopes for a quick settlement in that it challenged the contention that the disposition of the Shantung question was a matter to be settled by Japan and China alone. Lansing thought this was a good beginning. He noted that Wellington Koo, the Chinese spokesman, had "simply overwhelmed the Japanese with his argument." Evidence that the Japanese were indeed disturbed by the American tactics came on January 29 when a Japanese official called on Lansing to offset the effect of the Koo presentation by an indirect threat of deteriorating relations in the event the United States continued its campaign.[12]

From this point, however, it was the deterioration of the American position rather than worsening relations with Japan which concerned Lansing. Further discussion of the Shantung question was postponed until April. What happened in the interim is too well known to be discussed in detail here. It will be sufficient to say that the powers discovered Wilson's determination to establish the League of Nations overrode all other matters. The discovery resulted in Wilson's being subjected to intense pressure to concede specific desiderata in return for support for the inclusion of the League Covenant in the treaty. Japan was affected by the bargaining. In order to satisfy Wilson's requirements, she accepted a League mandate over the German islands instead of the outright control which she requested, and she abandoned her effort to have a clause providing for racial equality inserted in the Covenant in order to meet protests raised by the British Dominions. These concessions enabled Japan to assert that she would give up nothing more.

[12] Robert Lansing, *The Peace Negotiations* (Boston and New York, 1921), p. 253. Hereinafter cited as Lansing. *Peace Negotiations.*

In the latter days of April she presented Wilson with a hard choice: Japan's claims in Shantung must be approved by the Conference, or Japan would refuse to support the League. Lansing was embittered by the President's allowing himself to be maneuvered into such a position. The United States, he felt, should never have allowed the League and Shantung to be connected. They would not have been linked had not the President placed the League before all other things. The League, Lansing complained, was a "plaything of the President's which he takes to bed with him" and a "veritable millstone about our necks."[13]

Ironically Lansing, whose isolation from the main stream of negotiations has been much discussed, was consulted frequently by Wilson on Shantung. By the time the debate began in April, however, the context in which the issue was raised sharply limited America's action. In the circumstances, the Secretary could suggest only two schemes. The first provided that the powers join in a general renunciation of spheres of influence and that German rights in Shantung be ceded to the five victorious powers, which would administer them jointly for China. If accepted, this plan would block the extension of Japan's "special privileges" into Shantung and would provide an opening for American investors.[14] Apparently this was the plan that Lansing had been developing in the months before the opening of the Conference. He appears to have hoped that Britain and France, which were fearful of Japan's expanding monopoly, could be persuaded to back the idea, but whatever chance for success this plan may have had earlier was now gone. Britain had sought for herself and her Dominion the direct cession of German territory, and she had argued for the elimination of the

[13] "The Japanese Claims to Kiau Chau and Shantung Admitted," May 1, 1919, Lansing Collection, "Private Memoranda." Lansing to Polk, n. d., Polk Papers, Lansing-Polk Cor.

[14] Lansing started a campaign to break up the spheres just before the Conference met. See citations in footnote 3, this chapter. For strategy employed in April, see "Secretary's Notes of a Meeting Held at Quai d'Orsay," April 15, 17, 1919; "Minutes of a Meeting of the Council of Four," April 21, 22, 1919, *For. Rels., 1919, P. P. C.*, IV, 548-584; V, 135-147.

racial equality clause from the Covenant. These activities made it inexpedient for the British to turn about and oppose Japan's claims. Britain decided to stick with her earlier commitments to support the Japanese claims.[15] Lansing must have anticipated this reaction, for he expressed no surprise when he was informed of Britain's intentions.[16]

Lansing's second plan, one in which he placed more confidence than the one just outlined, called for independent American action to prevent Japan's writing her claims into the treaty. Wilson was to be persuaded that he must make no concessions to the Japanese. To do this every argument was presented to the President. It was emphasized that under Japanese control Shantung would provide a center from which Japan's claims to "special privilege" would radiate over much of central China. The Shantung Railway, for example, could easily be connected to China's trunk lines; thus Japan could gain the means for controlling much of China's trade.[17] Great emphasis was also placed on the unacceptability of the Japanese claims on moral grounds. The establishment of Japan's "special privilege" in Shantung would violate historic American policy and the principles embodied in Wilson's statements of American war aims. The arguments on these latter points reached a peak on April 29, the eve of the Shantung decision. Lansing, who knew of Wilson's admiration for General Tasker Bliss, asked Bliss to write Wilson on behalf of the American Peace Commissioners. The letter read in part:

> If it be right for a policeman, who recovers your purse, to keep the contents and claim that he has fulfilled his duty in returning the empty purse, then Japan's conduct may be tolerated.

[15] "Minutes of a Meeting of the Council of Four," April 25, 1919, *For. Rels., 1919, P. P. C.*, V, 246.

[16] Williams was informed on April 2, 1919, that the British and French delegates would uphold their obligations to Japan. SD PPC 185.1158/59.

[17] Wellington Koo Memorandum, n.d. This was transmitted to Wilson on April 12, 1919, with Lansing's comment that it showed "very clearly the international importance of Tsingtao, whose railway connections will make it the chief port of north China, and the injury to European and American trade already wrought by the temporary occupation of the port by Japan." SD PPC 185.1158/64a.

If it be right for Japan to annex the territory of an Ally, then it cannot be wrong for Italy to retain Fiume taken from the enemy.

If we support Japan's claim, we abandon the democracy of China to the domination of the Prussianized militarism of Japan.

We shall be sowing dragons teeth.

It can't be right to do wrong even to make peace. Peace is desirable, but there are things dearer than peace, justice and freedom.[18]

These arguments, which were carefully shaped to make the maximum impact on the President, were intended to do one thing: Wilson was to be persuaded that defeat of Japan's aspirations was more important than having Japan in the League. Lansing and his fellow Commissioners, White and Bliss, were themselves convinced of this. The three men agreed that the presence of a "Prussianized state" in the League would be likely to have a destructive effect on the organization. White and Bliss also concurred with Lansing in the idea that firm American resistance to the Japanese claims might ultimately diminish the prestige of Japan's militarists. Thus, they advised Wilson that the United States would gain nothing and lose much from any concessions to the Japanese views.[19]

[18] The Library of Congress, The Papers of Henry White, Box 4. Accounts of the events leading to the drafting of the letter are given by Bliss in a journal entry, April 29, 1919, The Library of Congress, The Papers of Tasker H. Bliss, Box 65, and a "Memorandum Regarding General Tasker H. Bliss," April 25, 1925, Baker Papers, I, 21.

[19] "The Japanese Claims to Kiau Chau and Shantung Admitted," May 1, 1919, Lansing Collection, "Private Memoranda." Lansing's views on the peaceful character of democracies were summarized in a letter to House, April 8, 1918: "The practical element, in my opinion, in any league of nations is the good faith of the members. If they are untrustworthy, an agreement to unite in the forcible maintenance of peace would be worthless. If this is the true view, the character of the membership should be the first consideration. . . .

"No people on earth desire war, particularly an aggressive war. If the people can exercise their will, they remain at peace. If a nation possesses democratic institutions, the popular will will be exercised. Consequently, if the principle of democracy prevails in a nation, it can be counted upon to preserve peace and oppose war.

"Applying these truths (if they are truths and I think they are), I have reached the conclusion that the only certain guarantor of international peace is a League of Democracies since they alone possess the trustworthy character which makes their word inviolate. A League, on the other hand, which

As is well known, Wilson listened carefully to these arguments and agonized over his decision. Ultimately, however, Japan was permitted to draft the articles giving her free disposal of German rights in return for oral assurances that Chinese sovereignty in Shantung would be restored at an unspecified time. Wilson believed that the concession was vital for the salvation of the League and that the League would subsequently right the wrongs done to China.

Lansing was outraged by the decision. On April 28, surmising what was forthcoming, he expressed his sentiments in his "Private Memoranda":

> Apparently the President is gonig [*sic*] to do this to avoid Japan's declining to enter the League of Nations. It is a surrender of the principle of self-determination, a transfer of millions of Chinese from one foreign master to another. This is another one of those secret arrangements which have riddled the "fourteen points" and are wrecking a just peace. I believe House is at the bottom of it. I said to him today that to give Kiau Chau to Japan was to barter away a great principle. He replied "We have had to do it before." I answered with some heat; "Yes, it has been done and it is the curse of this Conference that that method has been adopted." He made no reply, but that may have been because we were talking across a corner of the peace table in whispers.
>
> In my opinion, it would have been better to let Japan stay out of the League than to abandon China and surrender our prestige in the Far East for a "mess of pottage"—and a mess it is. I fear that it is too late to do anything to save the situation.

When Lansing learned two days later that his suspicions were correct, he added the postscript, "I believe that he [Wilson] will regret this one of these days."[20]

The language of this memorandum, like many others produced by Lansing at Paris, was unusually intemperate. This was

numbers among its members autocratic governments, possesses the elements of personal ambition, of intrigue and discord, which are the seeds of future wars."—Charles Seymore, ed., *The Intimate Papers of Colonel House* (Boston, 1926-1928), IV, 12-15.

[20] "Japanese Claims and the League of Nations," Lansing Collection, "Private Memoranda."

partly due to the Secretary's weariness and ill health. During early May Lansing asked Wilson's permission to go to London for a rest. His health, he feared, would break completely unless he left Paris.[21] Undoubtedly his condition arose as much from emotional as from organic causes. He was greatly agitated by the restrictions under which he worked. He had gone to Paris expecting sharp disagreements with the President. Indeed, the prospect caused him to tell his friends in Watertown that he might resign.[22] His failure to do so may be attributed to a desire to avoid embarrassing Wilson in advance of the peace negotiations and a conviction that he could indirectly influence the President's decisions. Thus, while Lansing was prepared to play a secondary role, he did not expect to be isolated from proceedings. Wilson's failure to consult with him and his decision to put House in charge temporarily of the American program were humiliations from which Lansing never fully recovered.[23]

But Lansing's distress over the Shantung settlement went deeper than these personal considerations. The President, he was convinced, had acted unwisely in at least two respects. A fundamental mistake was Wilson's bargaining for support of the League of Nations. Lansing's view of the League differed sharply from Wilson's. Lansing could not agree that the League offered the best hope for peace. To him, the plan seemed full of flaws. As an international lawyer who looked to the development of peace through world law, the idea of the great powers imposing their will on nations was objectionable. The League,

[21] Lansing to Wilson, May 9, 1919, *For. Rels., 1919, P. P. C.,* XI, 569.

[22] W. C. Stebbins to Lansing, July 28, 1919, Lansing Collection. Lansing, *Peace Negotiations,* pp. 187-189.

[23] The Shantung question was initially before the Council of Ten on which Lansing held a seat. After Wilson's return from Washington the discussion was confined to the Council of Four, from which Lansing was excluded. Lansing's Desk Diary (Lansing Collection) for April 4, 1919 contains this reference to the Secretary's exclusion from the highest councils: "I need not express my feelings. If it were not for the critical state of affairs and popular temper, I would ask to be allowed to return home. Patriotism and personal indignation are pulling in opposite directions. I suppose my sense of duty will swallow my pride."

moreover, was a novel organization, one which history suggested would not be supported enthusiastically by its members. The United States provided a good example of this. The long-established tradition of independent American action would make it extremely difficult for Wilson to win support for a plan wherein the United States committed itself in advance to apply sanctions to preserve the integrity of another state. In this respect Lansing was not particularly surprised by the warnings which had issued from the United States Senate. That these were inspired partly by partisan considerations he had no doubt, but he was equally convinced that Henry Cabot Lodge's group had much wisdom on its side. The League presented much too sharp a break with America's past for the United States to function in it as Wilson planned. Finally, the League seemed unwise from the standpoint of American security. Article X of the Convenant opened the way for the use of European forces in the Western Hemisphere. For one who had long emphasized the importance of American leadership in this area, such a breach of historic policy was unthinkable.[24]

These objections to the League must not be viewed as evidence of an isolationist spirit. The necessities of international life, Lansing believed, would require the United States to play an active, indeed, major, role in world affairs. He did not regard World War I as a moral crusade which would end with the elimination of the Kaiser. To be sure, the war had ideological aspects. The defeat of ambitious, militaristic states would relieve a threat to democratic government in the United States and elsewhere, but when stripped of these overtones, the war could be seen as an attempt to maintain a balance of power which was favorable to the entire scale of American interests. In order to meet Germany's threat to this balance of power, Lansing helped to shape American neutrality policies to favor Britain and

[24] Convenient critiques by Lansing of the League are contained in his *Peace Negotiations* and *The Big Four and Others of the Peace Conference* (Boston, 1921).

France and pressed for America's entry into the war.[25] Now that the Central Powers were defeated, the United States would need to remain alert for similar challenges from other sources. Lansing's effort to check extreme Japanese ambitions, for example, was evidence of an awareness that American security was related to the power balance in Asia as well as in Europe.

The issue between Lansing and Wilson, then, was the way in which the United States would discharge its international responsibilities. Lansing objected to the League of Nations because it was based on untested principles and was unlikely to achieve the results intended by its sponsors. As a substitute for the League, Lansing favored the establishment of new organs for the settlement of international dispute through arbitration and adjudication. The establishment of such organs would be accompanied by measures bringing nations under pressure to make use of them. This approach to peace, Lansing maintained, would enable the United States to maintain in its diplomacy a degree of flexibility which would be denied by membership in the League, would be supported by precedent indicating that the plan might work, and would not require the United States to give up valuable interests in order to obtain international support for its plans.[26]

According to Lansing, Wilson's second—and most profound—mistake was made after the League Covenant was drafted. The Secretary was convinced that Wilson should have forced a showdown when Japan threatened to leave the Conference in April. The Japanese, Lansing argued, were bluffing. Japan had only recently assumed the status of a great power, and her claim to that status was by no means assured. Therefore, Japan's desire for a place on the Council of the League, a position which would provide tangible evidence of her standing

[25] A recent stimulating study of Lansing's role in shaping American policy is Daniel M. Smith, *Robert Lansing and American Neutrality, 1914-1917* (Berkeley and Los Angeles, 1958). For a statement by Lansing on the need for future American participation in world politics, see his *Peace Negotiations,* p. 31.

[26] Lansing, *Peace Negotiations,* pp. 28-47.

among the powers, would prevent her from carrying out her threat not to sign the treaties and join the League. Recent research reveals that Lansing, in making this estimate, was wrong. The Japanese delegates did indeed have instructions to come home if their terms were not met. It must be remembered, however, that Lansing was willing to accept Japan's departure. While the Secretary did not explain this view, his reasoning may be surmised. The prospect that a Japanese victory on Shantung would enhance the militarists' prestige in Tokyo made it inexpedient to bargain for Japan's entry into the League. As a League member, Japan would be in an excellent spot to block any moves to curb her activities. Outside the League, the Japanese government was likely to come under strong pressure. This pressure would be exerted from within by businessmen and bankers who would be adversely affected by their country's declining relations with the West. It would also be exerted by powers, such as the United States, Britain, and France, which would co-operate to prevent Japan's infringing on their interests.[27] In a word, if Japan were to be controlled by militarists, American interests would be served best by Japan's remaining out of the League. This view opposed Wilson's, which presumed that the League would not be effective without Japanese participation.

In retrospect, striking parallels appear between events leading to the Lansing-Ishii talks and Shantung controversy. Prior to both occasions Lansing fashioned careful plans for the adjustment of American-Japanese difficulties, only to discover that he would not be permitted to try them. In 1917 and 1919 Wilson applied his own formulas and achieved some gains. The value of the Lansing-Ishii exchange has been noted. The Shantung settlement, insofar as it provided a basis for future

[27] It was generally assumed in the department that Japan was sensitive to world opinion. For example, Williams commented on America's exposure of Japan's attempts to force China to abandon her claims at Paris by saying the publicity did "lots of good" and "there's nothing like public criticism to control the Japanese." Williams to Long, Feb. 21; March 6, 1919, Long Papers.

international discussion of Japan's position in the province, gave China safeguards against unilateral Japanese action and represented a defeat for Japan's claims that western powers must not interfere in her dealings with China. In neither case, however, did Wilson accomplish as much as he hoped. Just as the Lansing-Ishii Notes failed to halt Japan's penetration of China, the League proved unable to modify Japan's dreams of empire.

A central purpose of the present study is to compare Wilson's accomplishments with the results that might have been anticipated had the President adopted the objectives and tactics suggested by Lansing. The nature of the Lansing-Ishii negotiations makes possible a fairly certain judgment. In 1917 the United States and Japan approached each other directly and not in conjunction with other powers; the negotiators were able to separate the issues causing the trouble from others confronting their nations; both parties were under pressures resulting from their participation in the war to resolve their difficulties; and finally, as a result of preliminary exchanges, a possible basis of settlement was outlined by Lansing and given tentative approval by Motono in advance of the actual negotiations. Given this information, the historian is on reasonably firm ground in suggesting that Lansing's program offered a workable alternative to the one adopted by Wilson.

It is less easy to appraise the plan proposed by Lansing at Paris. The Shantung question became entangled with the League of Nations; thus a question of whether the League were not more important than an immediate settlement with Japan was raised. Another difficulty appeared in Lansing's anticipation of British assistance. The Secretary apparently knew about the secret treaties, but he persisted in thinking that the British could be persuaded to side with the United States in violation of their treaty pledge. Ten years earlier Secretary Philander Knox had made a similar assumption in planning the neutralization of Manchurian railways. The British rejection of Knox's scheme could not have inspired in Lansing's mind absolute confidence in his own plan. (The Secretary's knowledge of the history of American policy suggested that he knew about the episode.) Nor in the time that has elaped since the Peace Conference has it been demonstrated that Britain's course would have changed had Lansing's advice been adopted. A third imponderable was whether Lansing was correct in assuming that a firm stand would result ultimately in the modification of Japanese foreign policy. Unlike 1917, when Motono stated unofficially what Japan would do in response to steps by the United States, Lansing based his expectations at the Peace Conference on the Hara Ministry's response to America's Siberian diplomacy. Hara's professed desire to co-operate on Siberian questions was encouraging, but the profession did not assure a shift on Shantung. In fact, by early April Lansing knew that Hara would face great difficulties in agreeing to return German rights and privileges to China. Japanese Army officers were reported to be ignoring their government's pledge of co-operation in Siberia, a situation which suggested that Hara might be unable to enforce any settlement embodying substantial concessions to the American view.[28] Thus, at Paris Lansing was conscious that his program might not produce the desired results. Moreover, subsequent investigations have failed to supply the information which Lansing lacked. In consequence, conclusions concerning Lansing's proposals on Shantung must be presented with less assurance than those pertaining to other aspects of his Far Eastern diplomacy.

Nevertheless, the record is sufficiently complete to permit some judgments as to the merits of Lansing's program. The first step is to view the differences between Wilson and Lansing in their chronological context. Lansing's initial criticism of Wilson's program centered on the high priority given to the drafting of the League Convenant. By pressing for completion of the Covenant, Lansing thought, the United States weakened its claim to British support without obtaining in return a satisfac-

[28] See Chapter XIII.

tory peace agency. A further result was that it placed the United States in the position of having to act alone in opposing Japanese claims. Lansing was distressed by these developments. It seemed to him that the United States had missed an opportunity to form a coalition which could impose effective restraints on Japan's ambitions. However, this was not to say that the United States was deprived of the ability to make a satisfactory settlement on Shantung. During the latter days of April, the United States was in a position to prevent Japan's writing her claims into the peace treaty. The move would not have resulted in the immediate withdrawal of Japan from Shantung, but it would have maintained America's record for refusing to recognize Japan's claim to "special interests." With negotiations on a banking consortium in the offing, it was likely that the United States would soon have the means for exerting effective pressure on Japan. It was Wilson's failure to block the Japanese attempt to place their claims in the treaty which caused the second major difference between the President and Secretary.

When viewed this way, the second major difference appears to have been the crucial one in determining the outcome of the Shantung controversy. Whether the United States might have enjoyed greater success at Paris had not Wilson given priority to the Covenant is an interesting question, but it is not the most important one which may be asked. Drafting the Covenant did not destroy American chances for a settlement on Shantung. Nor was the Covenant an issue between Wilson and Lansing when the Shantung settlement was made. It follows, therefore, that an appraisal of American diplomacy rests primarily on a judgment of whether Wilson was correct in making concessions to Japan.

Lansing's view was that the President's decision served the best interests of neither the United States nor Japan. As even a casual reading of the Secretary's writings shows, this was not a dispassionate opinion. Lansing's emotions were involved with the Shantung question. Wilson's decision to ignore his Secretary's advice reflected unfavorably on Lansing's prestige. Lansing was further alarmed by the thought that Wilson was encouraging militarism in Japan. Such a thought touched emotions which had been worn thin by the war. As a result, Lansing tended perhaps to attach too much importance to the Shantung question. For example, his theory that American concessions would place Japan immediately in the hands of militarists was not supported by subsequent events. Japan remained under moderate elements for a little more than a decade. In other respects, however, it must be recognized that Lansing's recommendations exhibited evidence of straight thinking. His analysis of Japan's probable response to alternate kinds of action was based on American experience in dealing with the Japanese in China and Siberia. That this experience was a useful guide for determining American policy was to be illustrated in the postwar years. If the Japanese government did not fall immediately into the hands of military extremists as Lansing feared it would, Lansing was correct in foreseeing the dangers to liberal government in Japan. During the 1920's, Japanese moderates were almost constantly under attack. The virtual seizure of power by militarists in 1931 demonstrated graphically the frail basis of party government. From this it appears that Lansing's emotions led him to underestimate the endurance of the Japanese moderates, but they did not cause him to exaggerate the seriousness of the challenge posed by the militarists. Again, it should be noted that China's integrity was to suffer further deterioration. While there were many reasons for this, one reason was the failure of the League to check Japan's push into China. Indeed, in 1931 the League not only was unable to stop Japan's conquest of Manchuria, but its inability to do so demonstrated its weakness to the world. The League was never to recover the prestige that it lost in the Manchurian crisis. Finally, it cannot be recorded that the Shantung settlement resulted in improved American-Japanese relations. The controversy deepened suspicions between the two countries. Thus, Lansing was able to anticipate some of the consequences of Wilson's decision. In view of this, the contemporary observer must at least question seriously the wisdom of Wilson's failure to heed his Secretary's advice.

Although Lansing was embittered by the Shantung decision, there was no time for recriminations. The peace had to be completed. Moreover, there remained important Far Eastern problems to be settled: consortium negotiations were pending; an attempt was to be made to commit Japan to a specific date on which she would transfer sovereignty of Shantung to China; and Japanese and American troubles in Siberia needed attention. In June, 1919, Lansing, who returned to Paris from his vacation, began a final effort to settle East Asian problems.

13. VAIN ENDEAVOR

The State Department's post-Peace Conference diplomacy covered no new ground. Viewed one way, it scarcely seemed that the Shantung debate had occurred. American diplomats worked on old problems using the same old formulas. Co-operation in Siberia and the organization of a banking consortium continued to be regarded as the most feasible ways of dealing with the emerging power of bolshevism and American-Japanese rivalries. And yet, the peace negotiations had left their mark. As Lansing had predicted, the Shantung settlement seemed to infuse the Japanese military with a fresh spirit of obstinacy, making the settlement of difficulties more troublesome than ever. On Americans the effect was reversed. The peace settlement was followed by a breakdown of morale and purpose among State Department personnel which was reflected in American diplomacy by diminishing energy and originality.

The ultimate deterioration of American efforts was foreshadowed by a tendency in the spring of 1919 to allow Siberian problems to drift. The inauguration of the interallied board's operations on March 5 seemed to have little effect on events. The board failed to keep the Chinese Eastern and Trans-Siberian Railways open to supplies which were moving toward anti-Bolshevik centers. Cossack irregulars under the leadership of the military adventurer, Gregory Seminov, continued their practice of stopping trains, diverting supplies, and exacting special levies. According to American observers, Seminov was encouraged and supported by the Japanese military. These latter appeared to resent intensely the power given Japanese moderates by the establishment of the railway board and were determined to thwart the purpose of the Hara Ministry by ignoring the board altogether. Furthermore, their determination posed a threat to the entire anti-Bolshevik movement. Not only was Seminov impeding the transportation of vital supplies, but his actions gave the Siberian populace reason to identify opponents of the revolution with the worst sort of behavior.[1]

Among American diplomats there was general agreement that Seminov should be controlled, but no one could think of an effective way of doing this. On March 23 the State Department resorted to diplomatic pressure. Kolchak was urged to assume responsibility for Seminov, and the Hara Ministry was asked to restrain the Japanese forces which were supporting Seminov's forces.[2] Almost from the outset, however, it was clear that these tactics would not be effective. The Kolchak regime was unable by itself to do anything about Seminov. Nor did the Hara Ministry display a willingness to act as the United States suggested. Nevertheless, the State Department failed to adopt an alternative line. The reason for this paralysis was given by Ambassador Morris. Discussing the link between the Japanese military and Seminov, he said:

> We cannot meet this conspiracy and enforce the "Open Door," necessary for the salvation of Russia, merely by frank discussion and formal protests in Tokyo. We must speak our determined purpose in the only language the Japanese military clique can understand [by raising American troop strength to the level of Japan's and using those troops to keep the railways open]. This will not lead to friction. On the contrary it will bring about a better understanding. We shall not only help the liberals in Russia; we shall render an even greater service to the liberal and progressive movement in Japan.
>
> The presence of a substantial number of American troops will

[1] Morris to Polk, March 8, 1919, SD 861.77/736.
[2] SD 861.00/4128.

serve to impress upon Cossack leaders and other reactionaries . . . the character and extent of the protection we are prepared to give American agencies.[3]

Here was the crux of the matter. Effective American action would require the shifting of additional troops to Siberia. Wilson, already under fire from the War Department and Congress to remove the troops which were already there, was unwilling to approve an enlarged program.

Lansing was irked by the President's determination. His desire to see the Bolsheviks crushed and Japanese military restrained was so intense that he was anxious to take all appropriate steps.[4] He attributed the President's unwillingness partly to his concern over the Treaty of Versailles. Wilson was fearful of taking steps which might prove unpopular and which would swell the opposition to the peace. It was on these grounds that Lansing opposed Wilson's whistle-stop trip to arouse popular support for the Treaty. The Secretary felt Wilson should accept the reservations proposed by the Senate, not fight them. Then the administration would be in a position to bid for Congressional support for an ambitious Siberian program.[5] Nothing, of course, came from Lansing's ideas. The breach between Lansing and Wilson widened during the summer of 1919. Working relations were almost entirely destroyed by Lansing's famous testimony before the Senate Foreign Relations Committee and

[3] To Lansing, July 30, 1919, *For. Rels., 1919, Russia,* pp. 29-34.

[4] The State Department had already taken the first steps in a new program to place restraints on the Japanese military. Part of this program was to avoid giving extremists any pretext for arousing public opinion against the United States. Lansing urged Wilson to refuse the Navy's request for permission to transfer some of the newest and heaviest vessels to the Pacific. Lansing to Wilson, March 22, 1919, Wilson Papers, VIII, 27. Polk privately asked American newspapermen to avoid criticizing Japan. Polk to Lansing, April, 1919, Polk Papers, Lansing-Polk Cor. An attempt was made to forestall Congressional action barring all Japanese working class immigrants from the United States. *For. Rels., 1919,* II, 417. During the summer, Lansing tried to win approval for the use of additional troops in Siberia. Lansing to Harris, August 12, 1919, *For. Rels., 1919, Russia,* pp. 412-413.

[5] "Need for Ratification of the Treaty is the Supreme Thing," Oct. 22, 1919, Lansing Collection, "Private Memoranda." Letters, Lansing to Polk, Aug.-Nov., 1919, Polk Papers, Lansing-Polk Cor. Lansing, *Peace Negotiations,* p. 276.

Wilson's subsequent physical breakdown. The result was that after August, 1919, America's Siberian venture was deprived of purpose. American troops remained in Siberia, but they were unable to control the breakdown of anti-Bolshevik forces.

Nor did the resumed consortium negotiations provide a bright prospect. Following the Shantung settlement, the State Department attached increased importance to the consortium idea. The controlling faction in Peking was reported to have regarded the action at Paris as a virtual western capitulation to Japanese aspirations. The war lords, as a result, were more disposed than ever to deal with Tokyo.[6] Only by persuading Japan to pool her loans with other powers did it seem possible to check the advance of Japanese monopoly.[7] Thus, the opening of discussions by bankers representing interested powers a few days after the Shantung issue was settled can scarcely be considered an accident as far as timing was concerned. Unhappily for American hopes, these talks, like the Siberian venture, ran afoul of the Japanese military.

The preliminary talks went well enough. American, Japanese, British, and French bankers reached a tentative agreement on operational plans late in May. The new consortium was to handle all loans. Upon joining the consortium, bankers were to pool existing loan options, and members were to obtain from their governments pledges to support only those loans to China which were made through the consortium. These terms would not only curtail the expansion of Japanese monopoly, but they would also deprive Japan of some claims already advanced in South Manchuria and Eastern Inner Mongolia. The State Department, which was delighted by the co-operative spirit of the Japanese bankers, began to speculate about an early conclusion to the negotiations.[8]

[6] Williams to Lansing, May 7, 1919, Lansing Collection. Reinsch to Polk, May 17, 1919, *For. Rels., 1919,* I, 350-353.

[7] Hugh D. Marshall to Long, May 20, 1919, Long Papers, "The Chinese Loan, 1919."

[8] Phillips to Reinsch, April 30, 1919, *For. Rels., 1919,* I, 511. Wallace to Lansing, May 23; Lansing to Wilson, May 26, 1919, Lansing Collection.

American confidence was retained during the first round of Japanese objections. When discussions were transferred from the bankers to the political level in June, Japan insisted that South Manchuria and Eastern Inner Mongolia be exempted from consortium operations. The move seemed to have originated with the same elements within the Japanese government which were insisting on an independent line in Siberia. Japanese banking representatives, on the other hand, emphatically assured American officials that they did not concur with their government's position.[9] This knowledge suggested the American tactics. On June 20 Lansing held a meeting in his Paris office for the purpose of instructing the men who were to carry the burden of negotiations. The Secretary favored sending Japan representations from the United States, Britain, and France. These would say that the proposed Japanese arrangement was wholly contrary to the spirit of the consortium, and if the Japanese persisted in their view, the three western powers would go forward without them. Hugh C. Wallace, who made a record of the meeting, noted that, "The Secretary was very strong in this stand. He felt that it would bring the Japanese in, rather than to prompt them to stay out."[10] From this it appears that Lansing was bringing into play ideas which he had hoped to apply earlier: a modification of Japanese policy was to be sought through pressure on important financial interests.

Whether Lansing's scheme would have worked at any time is a matter for speculation. The only certainty is that by the summer of 1919 its chances were much less favorable than they had been. The Wilson administration itself had lost much of its vigor. Remaining energies were directed primarily toward demobilizing and winning Senate approval of the peace treaty. Britain and France were affected by similar lethargy. The British government approved Lansing's plans in principle. Americans were conceded the right to enter the British sphere of

[9] John W. Davis to Polk, June 18, 1919, *For. Rels., 1919,* I, 451-452.
[10] Wallace to Polk, June 21, 1919, *For. Rels., 1919,* I, 453-454.

influence. Britain was prepared to join the United States in exerting pressure on Japan through the interallied railway board and consortium. Yet, the British government, like the Wilson administration, seemed unable to make decisions on essential details. For example, the British haggled over the proposal to extend government support only to consortium projects. Britain did not want to limit her business in China to the firms which belonged to the consortium. Debate on this issue, which dragged along for several weeks, prevented the United States and Britain from assuming a common front against Japan. France also contributed to western disunity. French bankers, who were occupied by pressing postwar problems, were mostly uninterested in Chinese investments. As a result, French representatives made clear their unwillingness to take a firm stand on any problem involving the consortium. Japan alone continued to manifest a strong policy, and this was in some measure due to the fact that the Hara Ministry had become increasingly responsive to the pressures of the military.[11] In consequence, the western powers failed to mount an economic offensive which impressed the Japanese government. The impasse on the consortium was not broken until the spring of 1920, when the State Department decided to meet Japan's demands. Lansing had dropped out of the consortium negotiations long before this time. Following the meeting in the Secretary's Paris office, Assistant Secretary Long assumed responsibility for the problem. Undoubtedly Lansing was aware that subsequent negotiations did not go satisfactorily, but he made no further significant suggestions before resigning from office.

The American failure to restrain Japanese action in Siberia or on loans to China contributed to still another failure on Shantung. Following the signature of the Treaty of Versailles, Lansing pointed out to Wilson that while German rights in Shantung were expressly transferred to Japan and Japan promised to transfer ultimately sovereignty in the province to China,

[11] Morris to Polk, June 15, 1919, *For. Rels., 1919,* I, 449-451.

the Treaty did not specify the way in which the latter transfer was to be executed. The vagueness permitted Japan to obtain from China privileges greater than those enjoyed by Germany. Indeed, the Sino-Japanese agreements of 1915 and 1918 indicated that this was Japan's ultimate purpose. Wilson responded to this advice by instructing the Secretary to seek a limiting declaration. The effort, however, was futile. The failure to make the railway board effective or to reach an agreement on a consortium left strong language as the only instrument the United States could use on the Japanese. The Hara Ministry was irritated by the American representations, but it refused any concessions.[12] In August the United States admitted defeat. Japan issued a public statement in which she evaded any commitments on the nature of the settlement to be made with China. To this the Wilson administration replied with a public statement giving its understanding of the oral commitments made by Japan at Paris.[13] The dispute was dropped at this point. It was not settled until the Washington Disarmament Conference provided the circumstances for the settlement of several outstanding Sino-Japanese differences.

In allowing the Shantung question to drop without an agreement, the State Department was simply repeating a pattern which also fitted the Siberian and consortium questions. Lansing emerged from the Peace Conference ready to continue to seek solutions to outstanding problems. Yet his energies quickly declined. This was partly due to the deterioration of his own position in the Wilson administration. Another factor was a general breakdown of government operations. On September 5, 1919, Gordon Auchincloss, House's son-in-law, noted that the State Department was completely demoralized. "It has no force left and those in office do no work," was his comment.[14] To

[12] The fullest array of documents on the question is in the Long Papers, "Memoranda, Japan, 1919."

[13] *New York Times,* Aug. 6, 7, 1919.

[14] House Papers, Auchincloss to House File.

which MacMurray, then in the Far Eastern Division, added a few months later:

> Nobody takes an initiative; the responsibility for foreseeing and meeting situations is not taken; things drift until they have reached the stage of being urgent and overshadowing emergencies that have to be met in some way. Some pray for the President's recovery, and some for the elections, but it seems as though the whole country were just prone and helpless and peevish that somebody doesn't hurry up and do something about it. The same spirit of restless passivity seems to pervade the whole Government; nothing gets done; nobody attempts anything; the answer to everything is "Don't start anything now." It is a numbing and disheartening atmosphere, and a bitter contrast to the purposefulness and high spirit of the days before the reaction set in.[15]

When viewed in this context, the fading of Lansing's activities during the summer of 1919 becomes understandable. The attempts to settle Far Eastern problems were going nowhere, and he knew it. There was no point in attempting to fashion new formulas; they were unlikely to obtain any more success than those already being applied. Things were simply allowed to drift. Lansing's bitterness was evident in the final entry in his Desk Diary for 1919: "E[leanor]. F[oster]. L[ansing]. and I went to church and saw the old year out. It has been a year of disappointed hopes."

In retrospect it seems that disappointments in Far Eastern affairs were confined to no single year. There was little to be accounted as an unqualified success in the entire span of the Wilson administration. The President was steadfastly determined to uphold the integrity of China. Available American resources were utilized to attain this end. But all that the United States could do appeared to have little effect on events in China. From 1913 to 1920 Chinese unity disintegrated. The regimes of "special privilege" were not dislodged. When Wilson left office, China's integrity was less intact than it had been eight years earlier. To these troubles may be added the growing American-

[15] To Morris, Feb. 7, 1920, The Library of Congress, The Papers of Roland S. Morris, Box 3.

Japanese rivalry which centered upon the question of China's status. The difficulty had not originated with the Wilson administration. The problem had been inherited. Yet the very intensity of the President's desire to assist China contributed to America's increasingly strained relations with Japan. Indeed, the breach was so serious that the settlement of American-Japanese difficulties became a major purpose of the Washington Disarmament Conference.

Historians have recorded these facts, but they still have found much to praise in Wilson's policy. The sincerity of the President's purpose has been admired. The key to Wilson's policy was his desire to use American resources to assist others toward a better life. The defense of China's integrity sprang from this concept of America's moral duty. Moreover, it has been pointed out that Wilson achieved considerable success in the face of overwhelming odds. American diplomacy was limited by the unwillingness of Americans to support forceful measures in the Pacific. In view of this, Japan's failure to obtain all she wanted during the Twenty-one Demands crisis and the Lansing-Ishii talks, and at Paris, reflects favorably on Wilson's diplomatic skill. While it was true that the President did not realize the full extent of his aims, it has been argued that China would almost certainly have emerged from World War I in a far more doleful state than was actually the case had it not been for the sincerity of Wilson's purpose and persistence of his effort.

When studied in the context of the goals which Wilson set for his administration, such conclusions have much to recommend them. The present study, however, has tried to suggest that the President's record may be viewed from another standpoint. Lansing raised important questions about Wilson's policy. Were the objectives set by Wilson in accord with basic American interests? Did the United States have the means for attaining its objectives? Was the defense of China's integrity of such importance as to risk growing friction with Japan? Or did expanding American interests in the Far East require an understanding with Japan as well as friendship for China? Lansing's answers cast doubt on the thesis that Wilson did as well as circumstances permitted.

Lansing's criticism of Wilson's policy stemmed partly from his understanding of historic American Far Eastern policy. In making the maintenance of China's integrity a primary American objective, Lansing believed, the President departed more sharply than he realized from precedent. As an objective in its own right, the principle of China's integrity had been accorded only sporadic support by the United States. Traditionally, the United States had been concerned mainly with providing the greatest opportunity for merchants and missionaries. The pursuit of these objectives had been largely responsible for whatever support the United States had given the principle of China's integrity. Support of the principle had not derived from much concern for China itself. Nor was the President correct in thinking that other nations had obligated themselves to support China's integrity. While the powers had frequently proclaimed their adherence to the Open Door, a doctrine which, they affirmed, included the principle of China's integrity, they had proceeded with the division of China into spheres of influence. Thus, although the United States had identified the Open Door with the maintenance of China's integrity, international support for the Open Door was at best confined to the pledges to observe certain nondiscriminatory practices with respect to foreign commerce that was conducted within the spheres of influence.

These considerations suggested that Wilson had at his disposal slender means for implementing his policy. Americans were unlikely to be aroused to support a defense of China's integrity which went beyond peaceful measures. The United States could not depend upon other nations to uphold the principle. And yet, having only the resources of American diplomacy, Wilson sought an objective which included a renunciation by the powers of their spheres of influence. Previous American efforts to persuade the powers to abandon their spheres had not met with success. By 1914 American prospects were scarcely improved, Japan had developed into a major power in East Asia, and she considered her claims to "special interests" in South Manchuria as vital to her national welfare. To Lansing it appeared that Wilson had failed to adjust his objective to the means for achieving it.

These considerations led Lansing to urge, directly at first and indirectly later, the substitution of other policy objectives. The United States should seek, as it had in the past, the advancement of commercial opportunity everywhere in East Asia. Support for China's integrity should be extended only insofar as it contributed to the advancement of this end or did not conflict with it. The principle should not be considered as an end in itself. Secondly, after 1917 the United States should seek the creation in Siberia of an anti-Bolshevik center. Thirdly, American-Japanese differences should be resolved and a basis established for co-operation between the two countries, this latter objective being also considered as a means for accomplishing the other two policy aims. These objectives, if realized, would directly benefit Americans. Business interests would derive profits from dealings with China and Japan; a beginning would be made in arresting the spread of the Communist menace; and a rivalry, which was becoming increasingly dangerous, would be resolved. At the same time, support accorded China's integrity for the purpose of safeguarding American commercial interests would satisfy in some measure Wilson's aim of aiding the Chinese.

To carry out this program, the United States must take two steps. The first of these was the encouragement of American business interests in China and Japan. This appeared at first to be an easy task. Trade with Japan was growing rapidly. With respect to China, the buildup of American investment capital, stability imposed on China by Yuan Shih-k'ai's regime, and prospective readiness of Europe to admit American interests to their spheres indicated that the State Department would need to do little to promote the China trade. When Yuan's regime collapsed and the powers objected to American entry into the spheres, however, the State Department responded with a carefully developed diplomatic program which was designed to assist firms having an interest in China. This program did not fulfill the department's early hopes, but it was not without achievement. By late 1917 American firms had obtained options on valuable projects, and Britain and Japan had admitted that Americans might co-operate with their own nationals in making investments within these spheres of influence.

The second, crucial step was for the United States to settle outstanding differences with Japan and to obtain Japan's co-operation in the carrying out of important American aims. In urging this step Lansing was constant in one respect. The United States, he believed, neither could, nor should, consider the use of force against Japan. Therefore, the American aim should be to encourage and strengthen elements within Japanese political circles which desired harmonious relations with the United States. Between 1915 and 1917 Lansing thought that this might be accomplished by striking a bargain in which Japan would pledge to raise no further complaint against America's handling of the land tenure question and to refrain from claiming monopolistic privileges in China Proper in return for American recognition of Japan's spheres of influence in South Manchuria and Eastern Inner Mongolia. Following the exchange of the Lansing-Ishii Notes in November, 1917, Lansing sought to assist Japanese moderates by bringing firm international pressure to bear on Japan. Such pressure, which was to be exerted through the interallied railway board, a revived consortium, and the refusal to permit Japan to write her Shantung claims into the peace treaty, would demonstrate to the Japanese the futility of ignoring the wishes of other powers with regard to East Asia and of attempting to monopolize that area for themselves.

Of the two steps proposed by Lansing, there was objection only to the last. Wilson approved plans to encourage the development of commercial opportunity, but he failed to sanction those with respect to Japan. The proposed bargain was unsatisfactory because it included America recognition of Japan's "special interests," an act which would infringe China's integrity. The plan to exert international pressure on Japan was opposed because it appeared destructive to the League of Nations. This failure of the President to concur with the Secretary on Japan constituted the chief difference between the two men on Far Eastern affairs. As it developed, it was a divergence of the greatest importance. One of the chief obstacles to the achievement of Wilson's aims was the development and assertion of Japan's imperial ambitions. An appraisal of Wilson's policy, therefore, must include a consideration as to whether or not these difficulties might have been avoided through the adoption of Lansing's program.

From the evidence presented in preceding pages, some things are clear. There were, as Lansing asserted, Japanese moderates, who were desirous of improved American-Japanese relations and who were willing to impose restraints on their own nation's ambitions in order to obtain those improved relations. Furthermore, these moderates were not only in a position to influence Japanese policy, but they were also ready to respond favorably to American attempts to strengthen their positions within the Japanese government. This was demonstrated by Motono's efforts to make the bargain which Lansing had suggested and by Hara's attempt to adjust Siberian difficulties to America's satisfaction. And finally, Lansing was correct in believing that the United States would receive support in its efforts to restrain Japan. Britain went on record in admitting the right of Americans to invest in projects within the British sphere and supporting revival of a banking consortium and organization of an interallied railway board. The British also appeared ready to help by persuading France to join the effort to control Japan. Thus, the record supports Lansing's contention that the United States had available means for making a mutually beneficial settlement of the American-Japanese difficulties and establishing a basis for co-operation between the two nations.

Such a conclusion does not lead automatically to the one that had Lansing's program been adopted, his other aims would have been realized. The Secretary was much too sophisticated a diplomat to believe that simple changes in programs led to large and far reaching results. For example, he was aware that the Japanese desiring a settlement with the United States faced powerful domestic opponents. This opposition made questionable the willingness of Japan to sustain any settlement in which valuable concessions were made to the United States. Again, Japan's threatened monopoly of China was not the only danger to American commercial opportunity. As the experience of 1916 and 1917 demonstrated, American investors were reluctant to enter China as long as there was no political order. While the Japanese had undoubtedly supported Chinese rebels, the State Department had no reason to think that a settlement with Japan would result in the restoration of tranquillity to China. Nor would a Japanese agreement to co-operate with the United States in Siberia necessarily result in defeat for the Bolsheviks. The Secretary recognized that to a considerable degree events in Russia were beyond the abilities of the United States and Japan to control. All of these and other difficulties of unsuspected origin were likely to arise to defeat the results which Lansing hoped to achieve through a settlement with Japan. Yet, in working for the adoption of his ideas, Lansing kept in mind the probable consequences of failure. To him it seemed that the gains for Wilson's policy were largely rhetorical. Wilson was succeeding in keeping open for discussion Japan's position in East Asia while permitting Japan to go forward with her attempts to monopolize the area and earning Japan's enmity for the United States. If the United States had adopted his programs, Lansing believed, the results would probably have been no worse, and there was a chance that much more might have been achieved. A contemporary analysis of the record indicates that this judgment was not far from the truth. During the Wilson administration, the United States missed at least two opportunities to reach understandings with Japan. It seems unfortunate that this was so. A settlement of American-Japanese differences might well have opened the way for substantial American accomplishments in East Asia.

Bibliography

The bibliography is divided into two major parts. Documents, manuscripts, and Lansing's own writings are grouped under Sections I-IV. These materials are located alphabetically within each category, and annotations are provided to indicate the usefulness of the source. Interviews, memoirs, printed letters, and secondary works are grouped under Section V. The titles included in this section are confined largely to works which are cited in the text and to uncited studies upon which the present writer relied for data and interpretation. The arrangement of these latter materials is varied from the arrangement which is used in Sections I-IV. Books are listed under the chapters in which they were used, and they are arranged topically rather than alphabetically.

I. Official Materials

Published:

China, The Imperial Maritime Customs. *Treaties, Conventions, etc., between China and Foreign States*. 2 vols. 2nd ed. New York, 1921.

Covers the period to 1917.

The basic printed record is the Department of State's *Papers Relating to the Foreign Relations of the United States*. While the volumes covering the Wilson administration do not contain many of the memoranda and interdepartmental correspondences upon which this study is based, they do provide an excellent sampling of materials in the State Department archives. The relevant volumes are as follows:

United States Department of State. *Papers Relating to the Foreign Relations of the United States, 1913-1920,* including *Supplements*. 15 vols. Washington, 1920-1934.

———. *Papers Relating to the Foreign Relations of the United States, 1918-1919, Russia.* 4 vols. Washington, 1932-1937.

———. *Papers Relating to the Foreign Relations of the United States, 1919, The Paris Peace Conference.* 13 vols. Washington, 1942-1947.

———. *Papers Relating to the Foreign Relations of the United States: The Lansing Papers, 1914-1920.* 2 vols. Washington, 1939-1940.

United States Tariff Commission. *Japan: Trade during the War.* Washington, 1919.

Unpublished:

United States Department of State. Archives, 1914-1920. The National Archives.

Contain a quantity of memoranda, interdepartment correspondence, and regular diplomatic correspondence which is not printed in *Foreign Relations.* From this material it is often possible to determine Lansing's personal views. Much of the data for the present study is derived from this source.

II. Official Documents Published Unofficially

Carnegie Endowment for International Peace. *The Sino-Japanese Negotiations of 1915, Japanese and Chinese Documents, and Chinese Official Statement.* Washington, 1921.

———. *The Imperial Japanese Mission to the United States, 1917.* Washington, 1918.

Provides a convenient compilation of published speeches, statements, and documents.

———. *Shantung: Treaties and Agreements.* Washington, 1921.

———. *The Consortium.* Washington, 1921.

Brings together relevant published documents.

Cocks, F. Seymore. *The Secret Treaties and Understandings.* London, 1918.

Gives the texts of Japan's treaties with European powers on Shantung and some Japanese comment on the Lansing-Ishii Notes.

"Documents Regarding the Chengchiatun Affair between China and Japan," *American Journal of International Law,* XI (August, 1917), 112-125.

MacMurray, John V. A. (ed.). *Treaties and Agreement with and Concerning China, 1894-1919.* 2 vols. New York, 1921.

A basic reference for the years covered in the present study.

III. Private Papers

Auchincloss, Gordon. Sterling Memorial Library, Yale University.
Contains a few letters to Colonel House on Lansing and conditions in the State Department. Nothing on the Far East.

Baker, Ray Stannard. Division of Manuscripts, Library of Congress.
Series I, which contains materials assembled for Baker's studies of Wilson, provides interviews, memoranda, and letters touching on Lansing and the Far East. The recollections of Lansing's Cabinet colleagues are especially useful.

Bryan, William Jennings. Division of Manuscripts, Library of Congress.
Two letterbooks contain copies of much of the Secretary's official correspondence. The items regarding the California land question and Twenty-one Demands are relevant to the present study. The files of general correspondence have a few items revealing the Bryan-Lansing relationship.

——— and Woodrow Wilson, The Correspondence of. State Department Archives, The National Archives.
More useful than the Bryan Papers in the Library of Congress. Four letterbooks deal with international questions. A few letters on Lansing's appointment as Counselor.

Bliss, Tasker H. Division of Manuscripts, Library of Congress.
Boxes 65-70 contain pertinent manuscripts. Shows the close relationship of Lansing and Bliss at Paris. Reveals only a little that cannot be found elsewhere on Lansing's views of the questions before the Peace Conference.

Daniels, Josephus. Division of Manuscripts, Library of Congress.
The Lansing file in the division, "Navy Period," contains a few items. Daniels' views on Lansing are given more fully in the Baker Papers.

Fortnightly Club Materials.
Held privately by Mrs. Seymore Jones, Watertown, New York.
A small chest of relics and correspondence. The latter bears on Lansing's relations with his boyhood friends.

Foster, John Watson. Division of Manuscripts, Library of Congress.
A disappointingly small and barren collection.

House, Edward M. Sterling Memorial Library, Yale University.
Only a few items of much importance on the Far East, but very important for Lansing's appointment as Secretary and his working arrangements in the administration. All materials, es-

pecially the Diary, must be used with caution. House seems to have had the historian constantly in mind as he produced his record.

Lansing, Robert. Division of Manuscripts, Library of Congress.

With the exception of the "Private Memoranda" and "Desk Diaries," which are important records touching on many phases of Lansing's official activities, this collection is composed mostly of personal correspondence for the years 1911-1928. These are valuable chiefly for tracing Lansing's career and learning about the man himself. The official papers which were originally part of the collection were separated from it by Mrs. Lansing after her husband's death. These latter items were turned over to the State Department, which published some of them in the volumes of the *Foreign Relations* series entitled *The Lansing Papers*. These manuscripts are now to be found woven into the State Department Archives.

In recent years there have been added to the correspondence in the Library of Congress several volumes of newspaper clippings which had been in the possession of Miss Emma Lansing, and the original manuscript of Lansing's *War Memoirs,* which was edited by John Foster Dulles. The former brings together fugitive material; the latter shows that the published volume is substantially as Lansing wrote it.

Lansing, Emma Sterling. Author's Files.

A small group of letters from Lansing's sister and his cousin, Mrs. John Gill, commenting on Lansing and making observations on an early draft of the first chapter of the present study.

Long, Breckinridge. Division of Manuscripts, Library of Congress.

An invaluable source. From 1917 to 1920 Long was chiefly responsible for the handling of Far Eastern problems. His papers contain many memoranda and letters which are not to be found in the State Department archives.

Morris, Roland S. Division of Manuscripts, Library of Congress.

A disappointingly thin collection. Valuable mainly for a few personal letters written during Morris' service in Tokyo.

Polk, Frank L. Sterling Memorial Library, Yale University.

An important collection. Polk and Lansing were close friends as well as professional associates. In consequence, the Lansing-Polk correspondence, though not voluminous, contains information which is to be found no other place. Valuable also for Polk's own record of his dealings with Far Eastern affairs.

Root, Elihu. Division of Manuscripts, Library of Congress.
Contains a few items which grew out of the professional association of Root and Lansing on arbitral tribunals.

Straight, Willard. Collection of Regional History, Cornell University.
Several pertinent items on the American International Corporation and investment in China, 1916-1917.

White, Henry. Division of Manuscripts, Library of Congress.
Most of the Peace Conference material in these files may be found elsewhere. However, Accession No. 9376 (Containers 3-11) holds some useful material on Shantung.

Wilson, Woodrow. Division of Manuscripts, Library of Congress.
Series II contains most of the Wilson-Lansing correspondence. Since the relationship between the two men was rather formal, much of their exchange was in writing. As a result, this correspondence is unusually rich.

IV. Lansing's Writings

Lansing's three volumes of memoirs have been important historical sources since their publication. No comment on the content of the individual volumes seems necessary.

The Peace Negotiations. Boston and New York, 1921.

The Big Four and Others of the Peace Conference. Boston, 1921.

War Memoirs of Robert Lansing. New York, 1935.

Lansing's other writings, of which there is a considerable quantity, have been less closely studied. Some of the pieces are quite revealing of the Secretary's thought on public problems.

His concepts of international law and the place of law in international relations are suggested in the following leading essays and reviews:

Notes on Sovereignty from the Standpoint of the State and of the World. Washington, 1921.

"The Newfoundland Fisheries Question," *American Journal of International Law,* III (April, 1909), 461-464.

"The North Atlantic Coast Fisheries," *American Journal of International Law,* IV (October, 1910), 903-908.

"The North Atlantic Coast Fisheries Arbitration," *American Journal of International Law,* V (January, 1911), 1-31.

"A Unique International Problem," *American Journal of International Law,* XI (October, 1917), 763-771.

"Some Legal Problems of the Peace Conference," *American Journal of International Law,* XIII (October, 1919), 631-650.

"The Trial of the Ex-Kaiser," *Forum,* LXII (October-November, 1919), 530-537.
"Can War Be Outlawed?," *Congressional Digest,* VII (March, 1928), 87-89.

For Lansing's views on the Treaty of Versailles and League of Nations, see:

"A Suggestion as to a Possible Policy in Relation to the Treaties of Peace and the League of Nations," *Outlook,* CXXVIII (June 29, 1921), 366-368.
"The Iroquois League of Nations," *Independent,* XCIII (October 4, 11, 1924), 222-224, 252-259.

An indication of Lansing's feelings concerning domestic reformers is given in:

"The Decay of American Parties," *Independent,* CXII (April 12, 1924), 193-195.

v. Interviews, Memoirs, Printed Letters and Secondary Works Listed by Chapter

Chapter 1. *A "Book Lawyer" Becomes A Diplomat*

Sources for the study of Lansing's life prior to 1911 are slim. Much of the data for his early years is drawn from three interviews, the records of which are in the author's possession: "Interview with Miss Emma Sterling Lansing, Watertown, New York, October 9, 1954"; "Interview with Miss Emma Sterling Lansing and Mrs. John L. Gill, Watertown, New York, August 30, 1955"; and "Memorandum of a Conversation with Miss Gertrude Helmer and Miss Nama Washburn, Watertown, New York, June 26, 1957."

The Lansing family and its activities is touched on in Alexander C. Flick (ed.), *History of the State of New York* (10 vols., New York, 1933-1937) and Edgar G. Emerson (ed.), *Our County and Its People, A Descriptive Work on Jefferson County, New York* (Boston, 1898).

There are several newspaper and periodical sketches of Lansing and his wife. Among the leading ones are: David F. Lane, "Robert Lansing as His Friends Know Him," *Collier's Magazine,* LVI (November 13, 1915), 23-24; Oswald G. Villard, "Two Counselors," *Nation,* C (March 25, 1915), 331; "He Holds One of the Hardest Jobs in the World," *American Magazine,* LXXXI (May, 1915), 52, by the same author; "Our Ad-Interim Secretary," *Literary Digest,* L (June 26, 1915), 1545-1546; "Robert Lansing," *World's Work,* XXX (August, 1915), 398-402; "The Diplomatic Counsellor General of the United States in Anxious Times," *Cur-*

rent Opinion, LVII (April, 1915), 239-240; "The Counselor for the State Department," *Outlook,* CIX (March 24, 1915), 658; "Mrs. Robert Lansing," *American Review of Reviews,* LII (August, 1915), 153; and William H. Taft, "Mrs. Robert Lansing, Diplomat," *Independent,* LXXXIII (July 15, 1915), 82-83.

The impression that Lansing made on Washington officialdom is recorded in memoirs, printed letters, and biographies: George Creel, *Rebel at Large: Recollections of Fifty Crowded Years* (New York, 1947); Josephus Daniels, *The Wilson Era: Years of Peace—1910-1917* (Chapel Hill, N. C., 1944); David F. Houston, *Eight Years with Wilson's Cabinet, 1913 to 1920* (2 vols., Garden City, 1926); Phillip C. Jessup, *Elihu Root* (2 vols., New York, 1938); William C. Redfield, *With Congress and Cabinet* (Garden City, 1924); Anne W. Lane and Louise H. Wall (eds.), *The Letters of Franklin K. Lane* (Boston and New York, 1922); Joseph P. Tumulty, *Woodrow Wilson as I Knew Him* (Garden City, 1921); and Edith Bolling Wilson, *My Memoirs* (Indianapolis, 1939).

John W. Foster's ideas on the Far East are in his *American Diplomacy in the Orient* (Boston and New York, 1903); and *Diplomatic Memoirs* (2 vols., Boston and New York, 1909).

William Phillips, *Ventures in Diplomacy* (Boston, 1953); Graham H. Stuart, *The Department of State: A History of Its Organization, Procedure, and Personnel* (New York, 1949); and Katharine Crane, *Mr. Carr of State: Forty-seven Years in the Department of State* (New York, 1960), provide insight into State Department operations during the years covered in the present study.

Julius Pratt, "Robert Lansing," *The American Secretaries of State and Their Diplomacy,* edited by Samuel Flagg Bemis (10 vols., New York, 1927-1929) contains some biographical material and represents the only serious effort to bring together the story of Lansing's diplomacy.

Chapter 2. *Questioning Wilson's Policy*

The interpretations of Wilson's policy given in the present study are drawn from several excellent volumes. A. Whitney Griswold, *The Far Eastern Policy of the United States* (New York, 1938) is a pioneer study which remains basically sound in its interpretations. On the genesis of the President's policy, Harley Notter, *The Origins of the Foreign Policy of Woodrow Wilson* (Baltimore, 1937) remains the best source. Roy W. Curry, *Woodrow Wilson and Far Eastern Policy, 1913-1921* (New York, 1957) is the only study of the entire Wilson administration and is the most thoughtful of those available. Tien-yi Li, *Woodrow Wilson's China Policy, 1913-1917* (New York, 1952) is useful for its discussion of the President's idealism with respect to China.

Ernest R. May, "American Policy and Japan's Entrance into World War I," *Mississippi Valley Historical Review,* XL (September, 1953), 279-290, is the basis for the statements on Bryan's views with respect to the neutralization of China. Information on Japan's decision to declare war is drawn from Charles N. Spinks, "Japan's Entrance into the World War," *Pacific Historical Review,* V (December, 1936), 297-311; Tatsuji Takeuchi, *War and Diplomacy in the Japanese Empire* (Garden City, 1935); and Russell H. Fifield, *Woodrow Wilson and the Far East: The Diplomacy of the Shantung Question* (New York, 1952).

Westel W. Willoughby, *Foreign Rights and Interests in China* (2 vols., 2nd ed., Baltimore, 1927); C. Walter Young, *Japan's Special Position in Manchuria: Its Assertion, Legal Interpretation, and Present Meaning* (Baltimore, 1931); and C. F. Remer, *Foreign Investment in China* (New York, 1933) are sources for determining the interests and claims of foreign powers in China.

For historical evidence which supports Lansing's contentions concerning the traditional basis of American interests in the Far East, see Tyler Dennett, *Americans in Eastern Asia: A Critical Study of the Policy of the United States with Respect to China, Japan, and Korea in the 19th Century* (New York, 1922); *Roosevelt and the Russo-Japanese War* (Garden City, 1925) by the same author; Charles S. Campbell, *Special Business Interests and the Open Door* (New Haven, 1951); and Charles Vevier, "The Open Door: An Idea in Action, 1906-1913," *Pacific Historical Review,* XXIV (February, 1955), 49-62.

Information on American-Japanese suspicions is drawn from Eleanor Tupper and George McReynolds, *Japan in American Public Opinion* (New York, 1937); Jefferson Jones, *The Fall of Tsingtao, with a Study of Japan's Ambitions in China* (Boston and New York, 1915); "Japan's Fear of a Chino-American Entente," and "Trying to Embroil America and Japan," *Literary Digest,* XLIX (July 25; November 28, 1914), 144, 1056-1057; and John H. Latane, "Our Relations with Japan," *American Political Science Reviews, VIII* (November, 1914), 583-601.

Chapter 3. *New Light On An Old Policy*

The freight rates controversy aroused little attention, and in consequence literature touching it is slim. Howard Ayers, "Reviving the Cotton Piece-Goods Trade with China," *Asia,* XVII (May, 1917), 219, gives the history of the trade. The viewpoint of an operator of an American shipping line on the Seaman's Bill is given in Robert Dollar, *Memoirs of Robert Dollar* (rev. ed., San Francisco, 1918).

Paul H. Clyde, "An Episode in American-Japanese Relations: The Manchurian Freight Rates Controversy," *Far Eastern Review,* XXVI (August-September, 1930), 410-412, 480-482, is a careful analysis based on published records. In this latter article and in "The Open Door Policy of John Hay," *Historical Outlook,* XXII (May, 1931), 210-214, Professor Clyde pointed out the limited nature of the Hay doctrine. These articles were the first to point out that the United States was inconsistent in its interpretations of the Open Door. Clyde's thesis has been developed superbly in a recent article. See Raymond A. Esthus, "The Changing Concept of the Open Door, 1899-1910," *Mississippi Valley Historical Review,* XLVI (December, 1959), 435-54.

Chapter 4. *A Proposed Bargain With Japan*

Willoughby and C. W. Young (cited, Chapter 2) provide information on Japan's claims in South Manchuria and Eastern Inner Mongolia. Ge-zay Wood, *The Twenty-One Demands: Japan vs. China* (New York and Chicago, 1921) and A. Morgan Young, *Japan Under Taisho Tenno, 1912-1926* (London, 1928) have information on the consolidation of Japan's position in Shantung.

In addition to Takeuchi (cited, Chapter 2), Delmar M. Brown, *Nationalism in Japan: An Introductory Historical Analysis* (Berkeley and Los Angeles, 1955) is helpful on Japan's expanding ambitions. Thomas E. LaFargue, *China and the World War* (Stanford, 1937) contains a standard study of the Twenty-one Demands.

For an indication of how deeply the State Department relied on peaceful means for dealing with Japan, see Paolo E. Colette, "Bryan Briefs Lansing," *Pacific Historical Review,* XXVII (November, 1958), 383-396.

William Jennings Bryan, *The Old World and Its Ways: A Tour Around the World and Journey through Europe* (St. Louis, 1907) gives insight into Bryan's friendship for Japan. Something of E. T. Williams' sentiment on China can be found in his two volumes: *A Short History of China* (New York, 1928) and *China Yesterday and Today* (5th rev. ed., New York, 1932).

Paul H. Clyde, "The Open Door in Relation to the Twenty-one Demands," *Pacific Affairs,* III (1930), 834-841, represents the first suggestion that American diplomacy was aimed primarily at the safeguarding of commercial interests.

Lansing's views on hemispheric security can be gleaned from Selig Adler, "Bryan and Wilsonian Caribbean Penetration," *Hispanic American Historical Review,* XX (May, 1940), 198-226; Wilfrid H. Callcott, *The Caribbean Policy of the United States, 1890-1920* (Baltimore, 1942); Dexter Perkins, *Hands Off: A History of the Monroe Doctrine* (Boston, 1941); J. Fred Rippy, *The Caribbean Danger Zone* (New York, 1940); and Charles Tansill, *The Purchase of the Danish West Indies* (Baltimore, 1932); and Louis G. Kahle, "Robert Lansing and the Recognition of Venustiano Carranza," *Hispanic-American Historical Review,* XXXVIII (August, 1958), 353-372.

Thomas A. Bailey, "California, Japan, and the Alien Land Tenure Legislation of 1913," *Pacific Historical Review,* I (March, 1932), 36-59, is a standard study. Dennett's *Roosevelt and the Russo-Japanese War* (cited, Chapter 2) shows that there was precedent for the Japanese effort in 1912 to strike a bargain with the United States.

Lansing's methods of dealing with Wilson are shown most clearly in his memoirs and manuscript sources, but on this topic Arthur S. Link, *Woodrow Wilson and the Progressive Era, 1910-1917* (New York, 1954) should also be noted.

Chapter 5. *The Counselor Becomes The Secretary*

Most of the memoirs of Lansing's Cabinet colleagues (cited, Chapter 1) contain comments on the appointment. One title that has not been noted is William G. McAdoo, *Crowded Years: The Reminiscences of William G. McAdoo* (Boston and New York, 1931).

Of the many studies of the relations of Wilson and House, Charles Seymour, "The Role of Colonel House in Wilson's Diplomacy," *Wilson's Foreign Policy in Perspective,* edited by Edward H. Buehrig (Bloomington, 1957), is the most suggestive. It differs in several respects from the interpretation given in the author's earlier *The Intimate Papers of Colonel House* (4 vols., Boston and New York, 1926).

Among the contemporary comments on Lansing's appointment, the following should be noted: "The Appointment of Mr. Robert Lansing as Secretary of State," *American Journal of International Law,* IX (July, 1915), 694-696; and "A Non-Political Secretary of State," *Nation,* CI (June 1, 1915), 7-8.

Chapter 6. *The Waiting Game*

Ernest B. Price, *The Russo-Japanese Treaties of 1907-1916 Concerning Manchuria and Mongolia* (Baltimore, 1933) remains the best analysis of the secret and public agreements by which Russia and Japan came to terms over their spheres of influence. A contemporary comment on the Russo-Chinese treaties on Mongolia by the Chief of the Far Eastern Division is E. T. Williams', "The Relations between China, Russia, and Mongolia," *American Journal of International Law,* X (1916), 798-808.

For differing interpretations on the origins of the Russo-Japanese agreements, see Pauline Tompkins, *American-Russian Relations in the Far East* (New York, 1949); and W. A. Williams, *American-Russian Relations, 1781-1947* (New York, 1952).

Putnam Weale (B. L. Simpson), *The Fight for the Republic of China* (New York, 1917) furnishes a contemporary account of the Chengchiatun incident.

Further evidence of American-Japanese tension is to be found in the following articles: "More 'Peril' in the Far East," "How Japan Views our Mexican Troubles"; and "Japan in the Doorway," *Literary Digest,* LIII (July 22, September 16, October 28, 1916), 172, 662, 1095; and "Alliance Directed Against America," *Far Eastern Review,* XIII (July, 1916), 56-57.

Chapter 7. *Dollar Diplomacy*

Paul S. Reinsch's concepts of the role to be played by business in America's China policy are given in his memoirs *An American Diplomat in China* (Garden City, 1922) and his articles "Slow Americans"; and "American Merchant Adventurers in China," *Asia,* XXII (February-March, 1922), 106, 186. A scholarly study of Reinsch's official career is Daniel Gage, "Paul S. Reinsch and Sino-American Relations" (unpublished doctoral dissertation, Stanford University, 1939).

Herbert Croly, *Willard Straight* (New York, 1924) is the standard reference on this promoter of American enterprise.

The *Far Eastern Review* and *Asia,* the latter of which was founded by Willard Straight, contain articles urging American investment in East Asia. The issues for 1916-1917 contain several articles giving information on the program inaugurated by the State Department. See especially the following: "The Grand Canal Improvement"; "American International Corporation"; Julian Arnold, "The New China and Modern Industry," *Far Eastern Review,* XIII (March, December, 1916), 366-396, 370-371, 797-799; "Should

America Co-operate with Japan in China?," *Asia,* XVI (December, 1916), 248-250; and Louis D. Froelick, "Building China's Railroads," Frank F. Davis, "Broadening our Chinese Trade," William H. Williams, "An American-Asiatic Business Program," Oscar E. Riley, "Notes from Japan," *Asia,* XVII (March-June, 1917), 5-12, 41-43, 132-134, 300-304.

Paul H. Clyde, "Railway Politics and the Open Door," *American Journal of International Law,* XXV (October, 1931), 642-657, is a pioneer analysis of Lansing's definition of the Open Door doctrine in China Proper.

Japan's economic growth is studied in several excellent works: Kakujiro Yamasaki and Gotaro Ogawa, *The Effect of the War upon the Commerce and Industry of Japan* (New York, 1929); William Lockwood, *The Economic Development of Japan: Growth and Structural Change, 1868-1938* (Princeton, 1954); and Ohara Keishi (comp.), *Japanese Trade and Industry in the Meiji-Taisho Era,* translated and adapted by Okata Tomatsu (Tokyo, 1957).

Frank C. Langdon, "Japan's Failure to Establish Friendly Relations with China in 1917-1918," *Pacific Historical Review,* XXVI (August, 1957), 245-258, summarizes the aims of the Terauchi Ministry. A brief analysis of the growing influence of businessmen in Japanese politics during the Terauchi Ministry is given in Robert Scalapino, *Democracy and the Party Movement in Prewar Japan: The Failure of the First Attempt* (Berkeley, 1953).

Feng Djen Djang, *The Diplomatic Relations between China and Germany since 1898* (Shanghai, 1936) provides information on the rights and privileges claimed by Germany in Shantung. A lucid narrative of China's domestic turmoil is Harold M. Vinacke, *Modern Constitutional Development in China* (Princeton, 1920).

Frederick V. Field, *American Participation in the China Consortiums* (Chicago, 1931) is the best reference on the subject.

Chapter 8. *China's Devoted Friend*

Sources for this chapter have been cited fully above. Of the titles listed, the most useful are Reinsch, *American Diplomat;* Gage, "Reinsch"; Lansing, *War Memoirs*; Vinacke, *Constitutional Development;* LaFargue, *China and the World War;* and Griswold, *American Far Eastern Policy.*

Chapter 9. *The Bargain Evaporates*

The most important printed sources are the writings of the men who were involved in the negotiations. Lansing's *War Memoirs* have been cited. Kikujiro Ishii, *Diplomatic Commentaries,* translated and edited by William R. Langdon (Baltimore, 1936) is a frank account. Ishii's views on the fundamental principles of Japanese policy are set forth in the article "The Permanent Bases of Japanese Foreign Policy," *Foreign Affairs,* II (January, 1933), 220-229. E. T. Williams, "Japan's Interests in Manchuria," *University of California Chronicle,* XXXIV (January, 1932), 1-27, gives information on the drafting of the Lansing-Ishii Notes.

Evidence that the Wilson administration feared a war with Japan is found scattered through the Polk and House Papers. Published comments on the subject include James F. Abbott, *Japanese Expansion and American Policies* (2nd ed., New York, 1916); and Frederick McCormick, *The Menace of Japan* (Boston, 1917). Iichiro Tokutomi, *Japanese-American Relations,* translated by S. Yanagiwara (New York, 1922), shows the growth of similar fears in Japan.

James W. Morley, *The Japanese Thrust into Siberia, 1918* (New York, 1957) provides valuable insights into the operation of Japan's internal politics in 1917. Hikomatsu Kamikawa (ed.), *Japan-American Diplomatic Relations in the Meiji-Taisho Era* translated by Michiko Kimura (Tokyo, 1958), gives Ishii's instructions but is disappointing in other respects. Takeuchi, *War and Diplomacy* (cited, Chapter 2) shows the Japanese expectations that a settlement would emerge from the talks.

Barbara Tuchman, *The Zimmerman Telegram* (New York, 1958) sifts the evidence on the much discussed German-Japanese alliance. A. M. Young, *Japan* (cited, Chapter 4) depicts Japan's lack of interest in the war after the capture of Shantung. Curry, *Wilson* (cited, Chapter 2) provides the best summary of American-Japanese differences over the Philippines. The development of Japanese pretensions in East Asia is shown in George Blakeslee, "The Japanese Monroe Doctrine," *Foreign Affairs,* XI (July, 1933), 671-681.

Chapter 10. *An Interlude Of Co-operation*

Among the works already cited, the following are the most valuable: Griswold's *American Far Eastern Policy* is outdated in some respects, but the interpretation of Wilson's motivation is supported by recent investigation; Curry, *Wilson,* contains a difficult but rewarding chapter on the President's views; Williams, *American-Russian Relations* points out the anti-Bolshevik sentiment of Lansing and his State Department colleagues; and Morley, *Japan's Thrust into Siberia* is an indispensable study on the formation of Japanese intervention policy.

To this list must be added three studies: Betty Miller Unterberger, *America's Siberian Expedition, 1918-1920: A Study of National Policy* (Durham, 1956) is the most intensive examination of the American record; George Kennan, *Soviet-American Relations, 1917-1920: The Decision to Intervene* (Princeton, 1958) combines the American, Japanese, and Russian records; John A. White, *The Siberian Intervention* (Princeton, 1950) is especially helpful on interallied diplomacy.

Chapter 11. *Return To 1909*

The titles cited in the preceding chapter are the basis for the continuing discussion of the Siberian involvement. On the consortium, Field, *China Consortiums* (cited, Chapter 7) is again a source. Data on the collapse of the Terauchi Ministry and accession of Hara are given in Scalapino, *Democracy and the Party Movement* (cited, Chapter 7); Chitoshi Yanaga, *Japan since Perry* (New York, 1949); Hugh Borton, *Japan's Modern Century* (New York, 1955); and Lawrence A. Olson, "Hara Kei: A Political Biography" (unpublished dissertation, Harvard University, 1954).

Chapter 12. *"A Veritable Millstone About Our Necks"*

Information on Lansing's health is derived from Miss Emma Lansing (interviews cited, Chapter 1), who was with her brother in Paris, and "The 'Most Likable' Secretary of State America Ever Had," *Current Opinion,* LXIV (June, 1918), 390-391.

Fifield, *Wilson and the Far East* (cited, Chapter 2) and "Japanese Policy toward the Shantung Question at the Paris Peace Conference," *Journal of Modern History,* XXIII (September, 1951), 265-272, by the same author, provide the basic narrative of the Shantung diplomacy, development of Wilson's views, and evaluation of Japanese policy.

Werner Levi, "American Attitudes toward the Pacific Islands, 1914-1919," *Pacific Historical Review,* XVII (February, 1948), 55-64, upholds the idea that Lansing knew about the secret treaties and shows that his attention was riveted on the Shantung question.

Paul Birdsall, *Versailles Twenty Years After* (New York, 1941) is helpful in that it views the issues at the Conference, as Lansing did, as being organized around the central issue of the League of Nations. The development of Wilson's attachment to the League is shown in Edward H. Buehrig, *Woodrow Wilson and the Balance of*

Power (Bloomington, 1955). W. A. Williams, "China and Japan: A Challenge and a Choice of the Nineteen Twenties," *Pacific Historical Review,* XXVI (August, 1957), 259-279, is suggestive on the choices open to the United States at the Paris Conference.

Daniel M. Smith's "Robert Lansing and the Formulation of American Neutrality Policies, 1914-1915," *Mississippi Valley Historical Review,* XLIII (June, 1956), 59-81; and *Robert Lansing and American Neutrality, 1914-1917* (Berkeley and Los Angeles, 1958) are cited here to show Lansing's concern with the dangers posed by militaristic states. However, the value of these studies is broader than the citations indicate. Using evidence which bears on American-European relations, Dr. Smith reaches conclusions similar to the ones in the present study concerning Lansing's place in the Wilson administration. Dr. Smith's findings increase the present writer's confidence in the conclusions reached in this study.

For the suggestion that the Shantung question should be viewed in the context of other Far Eastern problems, the writer is indebted to Professor Harry Harvin, Jr. See Harvin's "The Far East in the Peace Conference of 1919" (unpublished dissertation, Duke University, 1956).

Chapter 13. *Vain Endeavor*

See the titles listed under Chapters 10 and 11.

Index